Autism Belongs

Book Three of the School Daze Series

Dr. Sharon A. Mitchell

This is a work of fiction, a figment of the author's imagination. Any resemblance to real people or events is coincidental. This story is for entertainment and information purposes only. The author assumes no responsibility for the strategies and suggestions described.

Other books in the series:

Autism Goes to School

Autism Runs Away

Autism Belongs

Autism Talks & Talks

Autism Grows Up

Autism Goes to School Workbook (coming in 2017)

Prequel to Autism Goes to School (coming in 2017)

DEDICATION

To those unique individuals who have autism and the families who love them.

To the dedicated and talented people at Autism Services.

CONTENTS

ACKNOWLEDGMENTS

To M.E.L. - the most wondrous beta readers ever. This book owes a *lot* to you.

Thanks to Rachel at Littera Designs for the cover art.

DR. SHARON A. MITCHELL

Prologue

He flew against the door, causing it to burst open just slightly, and then slam shut again. He backed up and flung himself another time, with the same results. Next, he swiveled, attacking the door with his back instead of just one shoulder. This time the door bowed a few inches, before returning to the latched position.

The woman on the other side of the door alternated between soft sobs and low singing. She crooned a lullaby, sometimes in English, sometimes in Spanish, sometimes in a language incomprehensible. "My baby, my precious baby," she murmured. Tears flowed freely.

Her head smacked back against the door with each blow. With her back to the door and her feet braced against the edge of the vanity, she fought to keep the door closed, the only barrier between her and her attacker.

CHAPTER ONE

Tomas grabbed his pocket as his cell phone vibrated. A half second later the ring tone sounded that could indicate only one thing - his wife was in trouble. Again. He wheeled the skid-steer loader to the side of the warehouse, fishing the phone from his pocket. Finger on the answer button, he raised his eyes to meet those of his boss.

Mr. Humber didn't say a word.

Tomas raised an index finger in the signal for "just one minute". Even the warehouse noises could not mask the sounds of sobbing both he and Mr. Humbly could hear coming from the tiny speaker on the phone.

"It's my wife," explained Tomas. "Our son...."

"I don't care." Mr. Humber's face belied his words. He paused and his expression hardened. "We all have problems, but this is company time. Once or twice, maybe we can overlook it. But I've spoken to you before about this. I said that if you take that phone call, it's over. Either get that loader moving or come see me in my office. I'll be watching."

The sound of sobbing was masked by an unintelligible roar, the smashing of glass and shrieks of "No!" Tomas hesitated only a microsecond then put the phone to his ear.

"Maria! Maria! Are you there?" He paused. "Maria, speak to me."

"Oh, Tomas, I am so sorry to bother you at work." Through practice, Tomas could make sense of his wife's broken words.

"It's okay, Maria. Take a deep breath. Try to calm yourself and tell me what's happening." As if he didn't know.

"It's Manny. He's mad again. I'm sorry. I don't know what I did. He just came at me. I thought we were all right, and then he just started in."

"I know, honey. It's not your fault." Tomas paused. How many times had he wondered the same thing himself? "Are you hurt?"

"I'm okay. It's just a bit of blood and it's stopping now, but Manny, he's so upset." In the background the sounds of yelling and pounding overrode her words.

"Where are you now? Where is he?"

"I'm in the bathroom, like you told me to do. Manny's on the other side of the door. I'm so sorry, but I think he's made new holes in the door and part of the door jamb may be off. He's pushing on the door, trying to get in. I'm not sure the lock will hold."

"Did you position yourself the way I told you to?"

"Yes. My feet are against the vanity and my back is to the door. It's keeping the door shut, but the door bounces each time he throws himself at it.

"And Tomas, I think Manny has broken many more things this time. He threw the toaster to the floor and I think some parts flew off. He's mad that I'm hiding in the bathroom, so he's throwing dishes now. It sounds like lots are smashed."

"That's okay. The main thing is that you're safe. Now, is Manny safe? Did you lock the hallway door so he can't get out of the apartment?"

More sobbing. "I, I don't know. I think so. Oh, Tomas, I just don't remember for sure. I try to always do that when you leave for work. Maybe I did but I'm not sure. Oh, what if he leaves? Maybe I should go out and check."

"No! Don't do that. Just stay put. Remember what happened the last time you went to check and I wasn't there? We can't afford any more hospital visits. And, we know he hasn't left. I can hear him in the background, so he's all right. Just stay there. I'll be home as soon as I can. I love you. Just wait for me. I'm on my way."

Tomas's mind flashed to an image of the deadbolt he'd placed on the door to their apartment. Just under the deadbolt was a chain lock. No, no, Maria would not have put on that latch. She'd only turned the door lock and the deadbolt. Otherwise, how would he get in to rescue his family?

Tomas clicked off his phone, glancing up at the window overlooking the warehouse floor. Yes, as promised, there was Mr. Humber watching him.

Knowing what was coming, Tomas drove the loader to its parking spot, shut off the ignition and plugged the machine into the recharger. He did his usual walk-around to ensure that his area was safe and he'd left nothing in the way to harm a co-worker. If he was careful and precise, everything would be all right. They'd all be fine. Squaring his shoulders, he trudged up the stairs to knock on the door to his boss's office.

The muffled "come in" came sooner than Tomas hoped. Mr. Humber stood behind his chair, a tidy pile of cash precisely in the center of his desk blotter. The edges were exactly lined up. An envelope with the name Tomas Rodrigues typed in large block letters was just above the stack of bills.

Unsure whether to attempt an explanation, Tomas waited. So did Mr. Humber.

"You answered the phone."

"Yes, sir." What else could Tomas say?

"You made your choice."

He knew it was inevitable, but he needed this job to support his family. Struggling to maintain his dignity, Tomas tried. "I felt I had no choice, sir. My wife, she was in danger. *Is* in danger."

"Tomas, we are not unsympathetic to your situation. It's tough. I know that. But we have a business to run here. We need workers we can depend on."

"I understand. And, I am a good worker."

"Yes, you are. No one disputes that, when you're here. But how often do these calls come?"

As Tomas started to answer, Mr. Humber held up his hand.

"No, don't answer. It doesn't matter. At first, we understood. Emergencies happen to us all. We didn't keep track. But then it became a regular thing. Once a month, maybe we could overlook, but this is the third time this week. And the final time."

"I know, sir. We are working hard to solve the problem. I..." As much as he'd like to, Tomas could not promise that it would never happen again. That drew his mind back to what was likely happening with his son and wife at that very minute. He calculated how long it would take him to run home. There were less people on the streets in the middle of the day, so he could be faster than when going home after work.

"I'm sorry, Tomas, but it's over. This has happened too many times for us to keep you. We need workers we can depend on."

Tomas winced. A man was to be trusted. He must live up to his responsibilities. If he took on a commitment, he would fulfill it. And now, he'd let down this company that had taken a chance on him when he first came to this country. He had failed.

Mr. Humber indicated the money on the desk. "Here is your severance pay. It covers the two weeks until the end of this month."

Tomas started to interrupt, but Mr. Humber held up his hand.

"No, this is the way we are doing it. To be blunt, you're fired. But we do recognize the good job you do when you are here, so we're paying you out to the end of the month."

Tomas waited a second then raised his eyes from the money to Mr. Humber's face. "What if...?"

"No, this is final." He softened. "Look, in six months or a year, if your situation changes considerably, maybe we will talk again, but I'm making no promises. There are other men waiting to take your place who are dependable workers." He watched the way his words affected Tomas. "Go home and attend to your family. We wish you well." He gathered the bills into the envelope and passed it to Tomas.

Neither man offered to shake hands.

CHAPTER TWO

Pulling out his phone to check the time, Tomas hurried out of the place that had given him and his family a good living almost since the day he arrived in this country. He'd advanced in both responsibility and pay through hard work and diligence. He took pride in doing a good job and being known as a stand-up guy. Now, his reputation was shot.

His steps quickened as he realized just how much time had gone by since Maria's call. Was she all right? Where was Manny and what was he doing?

Tomas retrieved the last call on his cell phone and pressed the buttons to check on Maria. No answer. Maybe in his worry, he did something wrong and it wasn't Maria he'd called. He slowed his pace and punched in the numbers one by one. It rang once, twice, four times, and then clicked over to voice mail. At least he heard the sweet voice of his wife, but she didn't pick up. Tomas slowed and checked the number printed on the screen. Yes, it was the right number, of course it was, and he'd heard her answering machine message.

The phone went into his shirt pocket and he ran. Maria would know how worried he'd be and answer the phone if she at all could. Or, she'd call him back if she hadn't gotten to the phone in time. Tomas took the phone from his pocket to make sure he hadn't accidentally turned it off. Nope, it was on. His pace edged up from a jog to a sprint.

The punch came between his shoulder blades with a force that sent Tomas into a nose dive. His chin hit the sidewalk, followed by his nose and forehead. One hand scraped along the concrete; the other protected the chest pocket that contained his precious cell phone, his only link to what might be happening at home.

The blow stunned Tomas momentarily and he didn't know what had happened. He turned his head to glance behind to see what he'd tripped over. That was when he noticed the pairs of sneaker-clad feet surrounding him by the entrance to the alley.

Tomas braced his hands under his shoulders to push himself to his feet. It didn't work. A foot kept him on the ground, a foot that planted itself almost directly where the punch had landed moments ago. Instead, Tomas raised his head, trying to make eye contact with one of his attackers. His gaze skittered around his limited field of vision to see if help was coming. No one. By late afternoon this street would be teeming with commuters heading home from work, but now, well, it was deserted.

"Dios mio," he muttered. "Que Dios me ayude."

"Huh, there's no help for saps like you," was the only reply Tomas heard.

He tried again. "What do you want?"

"Your money, genius, what do you think?"

"I don't have any money. I just lost my job today. I'm broke."

"Riiight. That's what they all say." His buddies joined his snickers. "Now hand it over."

"I told you. I don't have money. I got fired, I'm telling you. I can give you my boss's name and you can go check. He's only a few blocks away."

"I feel a nap coming on and Joey here, well, he's got a thirst on. We need your cash and anything else interesting from your pockets."

The toe of the sneaker by Tomas's right ear tapped on the sidewalk. Its owner said, "Now we can do this nice and easy or we can do it the hard way."

"What do you mean?"

"Is he dense or what?" His buddies laughed with him. "You can nicely hand us everything that's in your pockets or we can take it from you. I figure we're being pretty big, giving you options here."

"I don't have any money."

"This is getting old. Have at it, guys."

Rough hands turned Tomas to his back. Unprepared for the move, the back of his head cracked on the sidewalk. One grimy hand felt the hard, rectangular shape in his shirt pocket and fished out Tomas's cell phone, waving it in the air.

"No, come on, guys. You gotta give that back to me. My wife, she's hurt. That's the only way I can keep in touch with her and my boy. I need that. She could be bleeding and unconscious. I *need* my phone."

"Ah. For a sob story, that's not bad, but we've heard better, right boys?"

Other hands continued their search through Tomas's pockets. One hand shoved the side of his face into the sidewalk while a booted foot kicked his hips over to follow his face. A fist dug out the envelope that was jammed deep into his back pocket.

There was the sound of paper tearing. "Well, looky, looky what we have here." The guy fanned the bills in the air.

"Please, that's my severance pay. I told you I just got fired. We need that. I have to pay the rent next week and without a job, that's all we have."

"Ah, you're breaking my heart, sucker. Here. The milk of human kindness and all that..." A five dollar bill fluttered to the ground by Tomas's shoulder. With one kick to his back, and one tromp on his hand, they left.

Tomas cradled his hand to his chest. Gently, he shook it. Bruised, but not broken. He used his other hand to help push himself into a sitting position. He rested his elbows on his knees and hung his head.

Now what? What was he going to do? A man's duty was to look after his family and he'd just lost the last bit of money they were likely to see for a while.

His family! How long had it been? He reached for his cell phone and reality flooded in. It was gone. What was he going to do?

As spry as a man at least twice his age, Tomas got to his feet. He held back a groan as he flexed his shoulder muscles and resumed his journey home. His urgency hurried his steps into a lumbering jog.

At the apartment door, Tomas realized with relief that the punks had not taken his keys. Thank God he kept just the two keys on a ring and they'd sunk deep into the corner of his front pocket. What if they'd taken his keys and he couldn't get inside to Maria and Manny? What if they'd found out where his family lived and paid a visit when he was not there to protect them?

Protect them. Yeah, right. A fine job he'd done of protecting himself. But what could he have done, he wondered, as he used the handrail to pull himself up the three flights of stairs to their apartment.

As he reached the top floor, all was quiet. There was no knot of fellow tenants huddled outside their door listening to the sounds of battle within. Once, elderly Mrs. Weymouth had even called the police.

Instead, all was silent. At least the door was shut.

It took only a few tries for Tomas' fingers to fit the key into the lock and turn the mechanism the correct way. As silently as he could, Tomas swung open the door just enough to get his head in. Carnage. Carnage and silence.

With a sweaty hand against the door, he pushed, still gently enough to make room for his head and shoulders. Not a sound. He entered fully, shutting the door behind him, all the while his gaze taking in the state of his apartment, the apartment his Maria tried to keep so beautifully.

His eyes landed on the couch and on Maria. There she was, her head draped over the arm of the overstuffed Goodwill find. Was she...? No, there was the rise and fall of her chest. These episodes with Manny left her so exhausted. But, her face. One eye was swelling shut. The trickle of blood over her eyebrow had slowed and was now drying in blobs and runs. Her cheek bone was swollen and he knew from experience that it would soon turn a plethora of rainbow colors. Oh, his poor, beautiful wife. She'd been hurt. Their son, the child she raised so lovingly, had hurt his mother. Again.

Manny! Where was he? Stepping farther into the room, he scanned the apartment. The space was small - a living room and kitchenette spot all in one, beside a galley kitchen just wide enough to allow two people to pass if they were back to back. Maybe Manny was in the over-size storage closet that housed the mattress where he slept.

Tomas started down the short hallway and there he was. Manny was asleep on the floor in front of the bathroom door. Drying tear tracks and mucous streaked his face. There was blood on some fingertips and bruising on his knuckles. One side of the bathroom door jamb was off, with its tip stuck into the drywall beside the doorway. Tomas cringed. He'd have to patch the sheet rock and somehow find paint exactly the right shade to match the wall, so the landlord would never know that their son had made a hole in the wall. *Another* hole in the wall. The jamb looked to be in one piece, so replacing that would be easier.

The open bathroom door allowed him to see the order and tidiness inside, telling him that Manny had not gotten to his mom while she hid, bracing herself against the door. Thank God. His Maria's injuries could have been much worse if the door had not held or if Maria had not braced herself sufficiently to keep the door closed against their son's attack.

It looked like Manny had exhausted himself and fallen asleep. When things had been silent long enough, Maria would have opened the door just a crack and peeked out, ready to slam it shut if Manny launched himself at her. Tomas winced at the thought. To think that a boy, *his* boy would hurt his mama. No child ever had a mama as good as his Maria. Where did Tomas go so very wrong to raise a son who could harm a woman, let alone his own mother?

Unwilling to wake Manny and risk an episode erupting again, Tomas tiptoed past. He noticed that the child was covered with a blanket. Ah, Maria. After being hurt and terrified by their son, she still looked out for him.

Gently, he leaned over the couch and pressed his lips to her uninjured cheek. She awoke with a start, hands up to protect herself, fear evident in her widened eyes, her mouth open to shriek.

"Sh, sh, querida." He placed a gentle finger over her lips. "It's all right. You're safe now. I'm home."

Maria raised herself up on one elbow. "Manny?" she asked. She tried to look over her husband's shoulder.

"He's fine. He's asleep on the floor in front of the bathroom."

"Ohhhh." Maria sank back onto the couch and closed her eyes. A tear trickled down her cheek. "I'm sorry about the mess, Tomas. I'll work on that in just a bit. I was so tired by the time Manny stopped that I needed to lay down for a minute."

"I know, I know. Sh. Stay where you are. We'll clean up together in a little while. Right now, I just want to know that you're all right." Maria moved over to make room on the couch for her husband. They cuddled together, relishing this quiet oasis in the turmoil their lives had become.

For a time, all was silent, and then Tomas asked, "We should talk about it. Can you tell me what happened?"

CHAPTER THREE

Maria's muscles spasmed in defensive mode.

"Sh, it's okay querida. I'm right here and Manny's still asleep. Tell me what went on."

"I'm so sorry. I didn't see it coming at all this time. I don't know what I did to set him off. I thought we were having a good morning. I was drinking coffee and reading a letter from my madre. Manny was at the table with me, eating cereal - dry, the way he likes it. He was picking up each piece with his fingers and seemed to be enjoying it. Then he stuck a piece in his ear - you know how he does that. I held his head, trying to get it out of his ear. Manny kept twisting his head and pulling away from me. He grabbed a spoon and started banging it on the table and hollering while rubbing the side of his head. He flipped over his cereal bowl, spilling it, which made him even madder. I couldn't figure out what was wrong.

"Then he yanked open the refrigerator door and started throwing things onto the floor. He grabbed the milk and tried to put it on the table. It landed partly on his overturned bowl and spilled. I caught the carton pretty quickly and set it down. I got a cloth and started cleaning up the mess. I kept telling Manny that it was all right."

Tomas nodded. Such incidents were not unusual.

"And then he ran to the cupboard, but tripped over some of the fridge stuff that he'd thrown on the floor. He bumped his head on the table leg and started yelling even more. Before I could get to him, he made it to the cupboard and got out the cereal. When I saw that he was heading back to the table, I righted his bowl and got ready to pour in the milk for him. That seemed to be what he wanted because once I poured from the box, he climbed back onto his chair.

"I thought the trouble was all over. He'd wanted milk with his cereal but didn't know how to tell me that. As he began eating, I put things back in the fridge and started cleaning up the mess." She looked up at her husband. "I'm sorry the place is still such a disaster."

Tomas pulled his arms more tightly around his wife and kissed her forehead just to the left of the rising bruise. "What happened then?"

"Manny took only a couple bites, and then got madder than ever. He threw his cereal bowl across the room, and his spoon. He yelled, and then he looked at me. Tomas, I know that look; I've seen it before. I braced myself like you told me to and got on the opposite side of the table. Still, this time that didn't help. He launched himself across the table at me. It happened so fast that I couldn't get out of the way. Plus I was worried that he'd fall and hurt himself. Falling on me would hurt him less than falling from that height onto the floor."

"Oh, my dear, I'm sorry I was not here for you."

Maria placed one palm along Tomas's cheek. "You were off making a living for us. It's my job to look after our home and child while you are out supporting us."

With Maria's words memories of that morning flooded back - the shame of being fired, then the indignities of being robbed. How would he tell this lovely woman who was doing so much for their son that he had lost his job? There would be time for that later. Now, he must be there for Maria. "Did he hurt you?"

"Oh, not so badly; I reacted quicker today. Honest, Tomas, I'm all right. It only bled for a while and the bruising, well, we know that that will go down. We do *not* need to go to the doctor or hospital this time. And, I think Manny is all right, although we should look at his hands. He pounded so hard and so long on the bathroom door."

"How did the two of you get from the kitchen table to the bathroom?"

Maria hung her head. "I ran." She met her husband's eyes. "I tried, really I did. I tried to talk to him. I tried to figure out what was wrong. I tried reasoning with him but he was just so mad. He kept hitting me and hitting me and yelling and punching, and then he tried picking up things off the floor to hit me with. I remembered what you said, how if Manny knocked me out, who would be here to look after him and what harm could he do to himself? So, I tried to get away from him and as soon as I could, I ran to the bathroom.

"Oh, did that make him mad. Remember the last time I did that? When he found that he could not get to me? Well, this time I think it was even worse because he remembered, I think. He used his fists on the door. It was so loud and so hard and the door actually moved when he pounded it. I was afraid that he was going to bust it open. He tried. He was so strong and he was furious with me.

"We need to check his nails; he may have hurt them. He tried to tear the jamb off the door to get in. He tried biting at the door knob when hitting it didn't work. I heard some splintering when he was kicking the door. That's when I called you. Sorry Tomas, but I thought the door was going to give and then what would I have done? I know that your boss does not like it when I call you at work but I didn't know what else to do. It felt like I was trying to block the door for hours."

"Querida, it is fine. You did exactly the right thing. We'll be okay."

Their conversation was interrupted by the sounds of blankets and clothing shifting against the hardwood floor by the bathroom.

Maria tensed and listened. The blankets settled down again. "Tomas, I am sorry to be such a poor mother to our son. I love him, but honestly, I wish he would stay asleep a bit longer. I don't feel ready to deal with him quite yet. Do you understand what I mean?"

"Yes, my Maria, me, too. I feel exactly the same way. Our Manny, he has become a difficult boy to live with. I do not know what we have done wrong. He has been a different child ever since he came into our lives, not what I imagined when we were expecting our baby."

"I am ashamed to say that sometimes I watch out the window and see the other kids there playing, or walking to school. They are the same age as our Manny or even younger. Yet, they talk. They can go outside and play. They go to school." Sadly, she added, "And maybe love their mamas. Maybe they don't beat them."

Tomas pulled back to look into his wife's eyes. He framed her face with his hands. "Maria, you are the best mother I know - wife and mother. Manny loves you, I know he does. We have some good times, don't we?"

Maria nodded, with some reluctance.

"Yes, we do. Our boy is not always like this." Although, it seems to be happening more and more often, Tomas thought.

They heard the sounds of Manny getting to his feet.

"Manny, my man, come and see your tata."

When Manny reached the couch, Tomas lifted him up to sit between his parents. Maria put her arms around him and their son nestled into her embrace. His warm, relaxed body fit snugly. Maria thought that anyone entering the apartment now would think they were the perfect family. But they weren't, she knew. Did other families hide such sad secrets as theirs?

Maria moved her hands down her son's arms. Gently, she picked up one hand and inspected it, then the other. Discoloration was beginning and those knuckles had to hurt. But from experience, she and Tomas had learned that Manny seemed to have a high tolerance for such pain. One of Maria's fears was that Manny would seriously hurt himself one day without his parents even knowing that it had happened. He didn't cry with pain. He didn't talk to them. So, after each such episode, Maria tried to inspect her son's body just to make sure he was all right. Physically. Secretly, she worried that something else might be wrong with her young one, something somewhere people could not see. Somewhere inside was something that could send her sweet boy on rampages.

Taking advantage of the mellow moment, Tomas relaxed with his little family. Why could not life stay just like this?

Manny squirmed and his parents released him from their arms. He started across the floor, almost sliding in the puddle of milk.

When Maria made to get up to clear away the mess, Tomas tightened his arm around her. "Soon. Soon we'll get up and start cleaning. But let's just rest here quietly for a few minutes. Manny seems okay now."

Indeed, he did. Looking at their beautiful child, you would never believe the tempest that had been Manny earlier that morning. It was always that way. He'd seem fine, then there would be a huge meltdown, then he'd fall asleep. When he awoke, it was for Manny as if nothing untoward had happened. But these episodes left his parents drained.

"Maria, I have to know. Did Mr. Toolan come? Did anyone call him or the police this time?" Mr. Toolan was the building's caretaker. Although initially patient once he realized that although he was nine years old, Manny did not yet talk, Mr. Toolan's tolerance wore thin with repairing the damage the child caused to the apartment. Months ago he had stopped fixing the things Manny broke; making it clear that the damages were the tenants' responsibility and Tomas must both pay for the materials and fix the damages himself.

"No. At least, I don't think so. I did not hear any knocking on the door or any yelling, but it was hard to hear above Manny's noise."

"Maybe none of the neighbors were home and there was no note on the door when I came in, so we're probably safe this time."

Maria snuggled back into her husband's embrace. Tomas hated to break this calm mood, but he had to tell her what had happened that morning.

Manny navigated the obstacles safely to where his blocks lived on the floor. That was *their* spot; they must remain exactly there or the world as they knew it would come to an end. Maria only ever washed the floor under them when they were positive Manny was asleep. She and Tomas would memorize the position of the blocks, and then replace them exactly as they had been. From bitter experience, they'd learned just how precise their son's memory was. He could tell if an angle or a distance was even slightly off.

The blocks went tumbling as Manny knocked them over, only to begin his endless game again. As he picked up one to join the growing stack, his gaze caught the sun coming in through the window. Dust motes danced in the air. Soon, Manny's fingers joined in the waltz, moving and swaying in the glittering dust specks. He stood, his body swaying to music that only he could hear.

"There goes our maestro," said Maria.

"At least he's quiet about it." Tomas's smile left his face. "Maria, there's something I have to tell you. I have bad news."

Maria examined her husband's face and noticed, really noticed for the first time the bruising. "Tomas, what happened? Did I black out and Manny hurt you?" Her fingers gently, so gently traced the discoloration on his forehead.

"No, it was not Manny. He was sleeping when I came in. This is worse."

Watching their son's graceful movements of hand patterns in the sun, he continued. "I lost my job. Mr. Humber heard the phone ring and fired me. He said it was one too many times."

Tears slid down Maria's face. "Oh, Tomas, I'm so sorry. So, so sorry. I should never have called you. I should be able to handle Manny by myself."

"No, querida. You did exactly the right thing. That was our plan, remember? Manny could seriously hurt you or hurt himself. He's big now, too strong for you when he gets like that. You were supposed to call me."

"But what will we do now?"

Tomas sighed. "Mr. Humber gave me two weeks' pay. Firing me was not just because of today - it's been coming for a while. He had an envelope of cash all ready with my name on it, as if he was just waiting for the moment to come."

"At least we're okay for a while then. We can pay the rent when it's due next week."

"No, we can't." Tomas didn't know which was the more shameful part to recount - the fact that he'd been fired from a good job or the fact that he'd then lost the last of their money. "On the way home I was mugged." At Maria's intake of breath, he was quick to reassure her. "I'm fine. I got a bit of bruising but they didn't really hurt me." On his other side, out of Maria's sight, he tried flexing the hand that had been stepped on. "I told them I had no money but they searched my pockets anyway and found the envelope with my severance pay. They took it - all of it except for this." He pulled out the rumpled five dollar bill, staring as he folded it over and over in his hands.

Maria turned and wrapped her arms around Tomas's neck. "As long as you're safe, we'll be all right. You'll think of something. It's just money. What would Manny and I have done if we'd lost you?"

Indeed, what *would* they do, wondered Tomas.

CHAPTER FOUR

Faint humming sounds came from near the window. This was Manny at his happiest. How could he go from pure, destructive rage, to being a cherub inside of an hour? His tantrums left his parents drained and tense and waiting for the next eruption, but they seemed to leave Manny relaxed and peaceful.

Although they didn't talk about it, Maria and Tomas each watched their son as they cleaned up the mess. Thank goodness Maria had moved their plates and glasses to the top cupboard shelf, making them harder for Manny to reach. They were down to just two plates, four glasses and three mugs; the rest had been smashed in previous episodes of Manny's anger. It would be harder to serve soup now that their son had broken their last bowl.

They worked quietly, or as quietly as a person could sweep up bits of broken glass and crockery. As soon as most of the shards were secured in the trash, Tomas grabbed his meager tool kit to see what he could do to repair the bathroom door. This time it was doubtful he could hide the damage from the caretaker's eyes.

At first, he tapped timidly with his hammer as he repositioned the door jamb, nervous that the sound of pounding might distract his son from the sun beams and start him up again. But Manny was so engrossed in a world only he understood that he did not flinch at the increasingly firm hits of metal on nail, or give any indication that he even heard what his dad was doing. In fact, it was like he was the only person in the room - possibly in the world, Tomas thought sadly. What would it be like to have a little boy who would run over excitedly whenever he saw his dad bring out the tool kit? He chided himself for wishing for something that might never be. He loved his boy, loved him exactly as he was.

As it tends to do, the sun moved in the sky. Tomas and Maria braced for another explosion. Sometimes, if Manny was not ready to move on to the next thing, losing his sun beams drove him inconsolably mad. This time though, they dodged a bullet and Manny left the window before the sun did. He wandered the room aimlessly. His parents watched him with uneasy eyes.

They couldn't just sit here, waiting for the other shoe to drop. Tomas needed to make plans; he needed a job. And, he needed to make things better for his family. Maybe he couldn't give them money right now, but perhaps he could do something to wipe that anxious look from his wife's beautiful eyes.

Before he broached his idea, Maria stood and held out a hand to him. "Come with me, love. I have something to show you."

Tomas let her lead him the few feet into the galley kitchen. Maria reached above the sink and took down the sugar container stashed at the back of the cupboard. It was covered with a thin film of dust; neither he nor Maria took sugar in their coffee so it seldom saw the light of day.

"Here," Maria said. "It's a surprise for you."

Tomas removed the small lid and inside was an assorted collection of bills. They were mostly small bills, but real bills, cash, nevertheless.

"Where'd you get this?" he asked.

Smiling, Maria explained. "I saved it, bit by bit. You sometimes give me too much money for groceries Tomas, so I save what we don't use. It's good to have some savings, no? I don't know how much there is, but maybe it will help."

Looking closer, Tomas saw that there was more money in here than at first glance. The bills were folded small and tight, allowing many more than you'd think would fit into that one, little sugar bowl.

"How should we celebrate?"

Maria watched their son. "Dare we?"

CHAPTER FIVE

"Let's go for a walk." Tomas knew that his wife had been cooped up in the apartment for far too long. When Manny was younger, she used to take him out often, but as he'd grown bigger and stronger and more unpredictable, it was no longer safe for her to go out alone with him.

Maria's face lit up, but then caution crept into her expression. "Are you sure?"

They both turned to look at Manny who was sitting on the floor spinning pot lids. "There are two of us. How bad could it be?" Tomas grinned at his wife. Yes, they both knew just how bad things could be.

"Why not? Do you want to tell him or should I?"

Getting him out of the house was easier than anticipated. Sometimes it went well, other times an abrupt change in routine was just not worth the effort. Manny was particularly sunny and cooperative right now.

Although dust motes were invisible outside, Manny still turned his face up to the sun's warmth. Fall was here and there would not be too many more days like this.

Tomas and Maria strolled along, careful where they placed their feet. From past experience they knew that the sound of crunching leaves sent their son off the deep end. They did not need to tell Manny; his footsteps automatically missed the fallen leaves, even when he seemed to be peering upward toward the sun's rays.

They walked the same route every time - had to. Any deviation bothered Manny so badly. When he was younger, he'd throw himself to the sidewalk, flailing and wailing if they tried taking a different street. Tomas would simply hoist the screaming child over his shoulder and they'd head home.

Now that Manny had some size on him, this was harder to do. Plus, strangers looked at a tantrumming two year old in one way, but a half grown child doing the same thing was an entirely different matter.

Once, when struggling with Manny in front of a house, the people inside called the police. The woman told the emergency dispatcher that a man and woman were trying to snatch a child. Two police cars roared up, lights and sirens flashing and parked in a V formation half on the sidewalk, surrounding Tomas and his family. At the noise and sudden appearance of armed men in uniform, Manny stopped his struggling and instead clung to his father desperately. Tomas stopped grappling with his son to hold him close, rubbing his back and saying soothing words over and over. It was Maria who tried to explain to the cops. When one policeman then another tried to get some sense out of Manny, they realized something was different with the child and backed off. After asking for identification, the procession followed the threesome home, one policeman coming up the stairs to check that all was as Maria said it was. As Tomas set Manny on his feet inside the door of their apartment, Manny ran for the couch, picked up the remote, and settled in to watch TV with the waiting blanket wrapped around him. He looked like a boy who had done those exact actions over and over again and the officer left satisfied that the couple was not abducting some strange child.

But, today the sun was shining, and Manny seemed content. It would be a good walk, one of those they'd look back on and remember fondly. One without incident.

Their neighborhood was shoddy-gentrified, an area not quite in transition. It was a mixture of single family, white-picket, small homes, older, low-rise apartment buildings and shops with owner-apartments overhead.

Although it never appeared that Manny paid any attention to where they were, he knew. Oh, he knew. The last few times they'd headed down this street, he had been transfixed by the display in the bakery shop window. Each time, it seemed harder and harder to get him to move on. Now, what to do, what to do? Should they continue on this street, knowing that they'd soon have to pass the bakery, or attempt to turn left at the next corner, *not* a move on their regular route?

At the corner, Tomas angled his body to make the turn. Immediately, Manny's arms came up at his sides, his hands elevated and that keening noise started in the back on his throat. His parents knew what this meant. Manny might not speak, but he communicated, for sure. At least, sometimes.

"All right, son. I understand. Papa made a mistake is all. We'll go straight." He pointed down the way they had originally been heading. Manny's noises stopped and he walked ahead of his parents on what he knew was the correct path. Tomas grabbed Maria's hand and gave it a squeeze. "Just hang loose and it'll be all right. Show him we're relaxed and we'll walk right on by."

Nope, not gonna happen. That's what Manny's body language said. He planted himself firmly in front of the bakery window and pressed his nose to the glass. He made little noises but not the ominous ones that forewarned of an eruption. These were more like happy noises, contented ones. If all their son wanted was a quick peek in a bakery window, then Tomas and Maria would oblige.

How long can you wait, nonchalantly regarding bakery goodies? Is it seconds or minutes before passersby notice or the bakery owner comes out to ask what you're doing?

Now Manny's hand rose and his fingers planted themselves on the window. His other hand came out of his mouth to join its partner. The pristine window became smeared.

"Okay, bud, it's time to get moving," said Tomas.

No reaction.

"Manny, let's go."

Still nothing. It was as if his son had not heard.

Maria scanned the street, checking to see how many people might witness the oncoming tsunami. Luckily, the street was deserted except for one couple, hand in hand, closing in on them fast. "Tomas..." Maria warned, with a nod toward the man and woman.

"I know, babe." He tried to put an arm around his son's shoulder to steer him away. Manny would have none of it and squirmed back into position. A glance over his shoulder showed Tomas that they were no longer alone.

"Hi," the woman said. Without waiting for a reply, she walked up to stand beside Manny. "Like what you see?" she asked him.

Manny ignored her. She didn't seem to notice or care.

"See that one over there?" The woman pointed in the direction of the cream puffs. "That's my favorite."

Still no reaction from Manny.

"But, when I'm feeling in the mood for chocolate, those éclairs really do it for me." She pointed to a lower shelf.

This time, Manny angled his body in the direction of her point.

The woman turned to survey Manny. "Let me see, young man. I wonder which one you like best. Hmmm. I have a nephew about your age and he, well he likes them all, but he especially likes the gingerbread cookies - the ones over there."

This time, there was no mistaking that Manny was paying attention. His eyes lit up and his fist banged on the glass.

The woman laughed. "Yeah, me, too. I get excited just thinking about eating one. It's just as well, since I'm here so often."

Tomas's distress was increasing by the minute. He gave a polite smile to the talkative woman then said, "We must be on our way. Manny, come." He hoped that he'd inserted just the right amount of assertiveness in his tone - just enough to get his son to comply but not enough to make him freak out. Tomas tried to wedge his body in between his son and woman. In case Manny pitched a fit, a stranger should not get caught in the crossfire.

The woman was not good at taking a hint. Instead, she turned to Maria. "Are you his mom? Did you know that this bakery gives a free cookie to every child who comes in?"

As this sentence started to unfold and Maria could see where it was going, she tried to frantically signal the woman to stop, to be quiet, to run away, anything other than say what she just said.

Manny heard. Of course he did and oh, he definitely understood what he heard. He turned to his parents with a grin. One hand remained flattened on the window and the other commenced flapping in the wind. His body tensed and his heels left the ground, then lowered and repeated the exercise over and over.

Maria and Tomas exchanged deer-in-the-headlight glances. What to do now?

Paying no heed to the body language of the parents and surprisingly, ignoring Manny's posturing, the strange woman bent, nudged Manny's shoulder with her own, then headed towards the door of the bakery. Looking at him over her shoulder, she said, "Come on. There's a cookie with your name on it in here." She held the door as Manny walked toward her.

So far, her companion had hung back but now he stepped forward. Addressing the parents, he said, "She's quite a force, but I can assure you, she's harmless. Honest. And, she likes kids. For some reason, she's good with them and they don't mind that she just blunders on in."

Tomas and Maria were like stone statuaries planted on the sidewalk, watching in horror as their son, their unpredictable son entered the bakery with a stranger. Shaking himself out of the reverie, Tomas glanced inside and cringed. The place was filled with tiny, glass tables and curved, wrought iron chairs. Visions of the shattered crockery in their apartment filled his mind.

The gentleman was still holding open the door. "You'd better go in," he said. "You might want to rescue your son from Ellie before she talks his ear off."

Inside, Ellie and Manny were crouched together in front of the counter display cabinet. Three of Manny's fingers were back inside his mouth, a good sign that meant he was relaxed. He always pulled them out before letting out a shriek. Ellie was pointing and naming each different piece of confectionary and Manny appeared to be paying rapt attention. Ellie finished with, "So which do you want?"

Maria stepped forward. "I'm so sorry. Everything looks good, but I forgot my purse at home. We'll have to come back another time when we have our money."

How brave his wife was, thought Tomas. She knew that denying Manny a sweet would bring about a doozy of a scene and still she waded in. "Querida, I think I have a few dollars in my pocket. We can get a small something for our little man." He'd pocketed a bit of money from the sugar bowl, just for emergencies.

The woman interrupted. "Oh, it's free for kids."

Maria looked from her to the man, checking if this could possibly be true.

The woman ignored Maria, her attention on the child as she followed Manny's gaze. "Got it. I see which one you want. Hang on a sec and I'll be right back." She lifted up the part of the counter that separated the customers from the staff and walked through, plunking the board back down in its place. She went to the sink to wash her hands, and then donned an apron.

As if it needed an explanation, the man pointed at her said, "That's Ellie. She owns the place. |"

Ducking down behind the counter to reach for Manny's treat, Ellie raised one hand in a sort-of wave.

The man raised his eyebrows heaven-ward then stuck out his hand. "I'm Rob. I try to follow along after Ellie and keep her out of trouble."

Tomas shook his hand and introduced himself and Maria. He indicated his son. "That's Manny. He, ah, doesn't talk much."

Maria looked at him. Much?

Meanwhile, Ellie came through another door with a plate in hand. A paper doily on the plate held a gingerbread man whose arms and legs splayed off the edges. Manny followed her with his eyes, bouncing on his toes. Ellie waved an arm. "Come one. Have a seat here." She placed the goodie on one of those fragile, glass tables and held out a chair for Manny.

He clambered onto the chair, bracing himself on the table for balance. The table started to tip, but Ellie caught it with her hip as if she did it every day. She slid Manny's chair closer to the table and placed a napkin beside his plate.

Maria followed along, worried. "Maybe he should not sit there. The table looks breakable and he can be, well..."

"Oh, nonsense," Ellie interrupted. "He's fine. My nephew sits at these tables all the time and if they survive Kyle, they'll survive any kid. Besides, they're safety glass. Come on and have a seat."

When Tomas and Maria warily sat down, they kept their eyes glued on their son, ready to spring into action if needed.

"What'll you have?"

Tomas realized that Ellie was repeating her question. "Just a cup of coffee for me please, and for you, Maria?"

When Ellie brought them their drinks, she included a malted milkshake for Manny. With a straw, in a tall, heavy, crystal glass. Manny's hands reached for it. Before either of his parents could make the save, Ellie swooped in. Prepared, she grabbed it and put it back in the center of the table. "Nope, that's for after your cookie. You finish everything on your plate, and then call me. I'll show you how to drink this." She paused and looked Manny in the eye sternly. "Got it?"

Manny's eyes drifted from Ellie to the milkshake then back again. He held her gaze.

Ellie gave him a thumbs up and smiled. "Remember; let me know when you're ready." Then, she was off.

Both Maria and Tomas sat with their hands on the table, at the ready to grab if things started to go flying. Neither took their eyes off their son or that milkshake.

Maria whispered, "A *glass* container? What was she thinking?"

The bell over the bakery door chimed. Running feet and a boisterous, high pitched voice announced, "Munchkin's here!"

Wiping her hands on her apron, Ellie hustled from behind the counter to catch the eight year old boy who sprang at her. "Hello, Munchkin. Just what did you do with my nephew, Kyle? I was hoping he'd drop in."

"I *am* Kyle, silly. You just call me Munchkin sometimes."

"Oh, you're so right. You do resemble Kyle. Did you bring your mom and dad along or did you drive over by yourself?"

Seriously, Kyle regarded her. "I don't know how to drive, you know. I don't think dad would let me try. The rule is that you have to be sixteen before you can get a license."

"You're right. I was just kidding you."

Kyle looked puzzled at that, but went to the pastry counter to peruse today's selections.

Giving Kyle's parents, Ben and Mel a hug, Ellie asked, "The usual?" Without waiting for an answer, she walked away to inspect goodies with Kyle.

Mel and Ben shrugged and shared a smile. They hung up their coats and sat at a round table with seating for three. After great deliberation, with input from both Ellie and Rob, Kyle slow-stepped his way to his parents table carefully carrying his precious cargo of his usual plate of giant gingerbread cookie. No matter how many times he visited the bakery and no matter how much deliberation went into his choice, he ended up choosing the same selection he had made the very first time he came here.

Rob brought over their drink orders, with a latte for himself. He drew up another chair to join them. "Well," he informed Ben, "your sister's done it again." He nodded to the trio at the other table that included a boy solemnly nibbling off the leg of a gingerbread man. "They were standing outside, minding their own business, when Ellie charmed the kid, leaving the parents no choice but to follow." He stirred some golden, coconut sugar into his latte. "Mel, you might be interested in the boy...." He left the rest of the words unspoken, but Mel got his meaning. They'd been teachers in the same school for several years now and had similar affinities to kids who learned differently.

Peace reigned as everyone applied themselves to their food or drink. The sounds of teaspoons clinking against cups and low murmurs of conversation floated around the bakery. The smells of cinnamon and fresh yeast breads overlaid that of the slow-roasted brisket that would yield sandwich meat for the supper crowd.

A howl broke the calm. Then the sound of a chair rocking on its legs.

"No, Manny, shh, shh, shh." Tomas was instantly behind his son, trying to prevent him from rocking the chair either over or into the glass table that was oh so close to his son's face. "Manny, stop. No!"

And, Ellie was there. "Well, I told you to let me know when you finished your cookie, didn't I? I neglected to tell you how to notify me though. Never mind. Your way worked just fine and here I am." She looked at Tomas and asked, "May I?" With her hip, she gently pushed the father out of her way.

"Here's the way we do it, Manny," she said as she leaned over him.

At her action, Maria drew in her breath. How many times had she been head-butted by her son when she got too close like that? She looked to Tomas and saw that he had the same fear.

But, Ellie carried on regardless of their looks or sputtered words. "Now, we move your plate out of the way and bring the milkshake closer."

When Manny reached for it, she said sharply, "No, not yet."

There was a sharp intake of breath from Maria. You did *not* say no to Manny when there was something he wanted.

"Now," continued Ellie. "We scoot your chair back a bit like this to give you room. Now, hold out your hands." When Manny did as she asked, she placed the milkshake on his lap and folded his hands around it. "You have to use both hands, like this, or it will spill." She came around to the side of his chair and squatted down. "Here. I'll move the straw the first time for you, and then you have to do it yourself next time." She positioned it next to his bent head. "Now, sip."

Manny didn't move his head. He stared at the frothy drink with longing. Ellie glanced at his parents. "Does he know how to use a straw?"

"I don't think he's ever tried one before."

Rob, watching the interchange had hustled over the counter and returned with a second straw for Ellie. She smiled her thanks at him. What a guy.

Ellie inserted her straw into the milkshake, took a big breath in, then, with exaggerated cheeks sucked in a big gulp of malted milk. Swallowing, she smiled at Manny. "Now, you try."

It took a few seconds of chasing the straw around with his lips, but Manny got the hang of it. His first gulp was so big, that the malt spilled out of his lips. Ellie grabbed a couple napkins and mopped him up. "My fault. I should not have shown you how to take such a big gulp. Try again, taking just a small sip this time." She imitated taking a little drink through a straw.

This time Manny got it right and the look on his face told the story of what he thought of his first malted shake. Ellie removed her straw and, wrapping it in a napkin, took it with her. "Enjoy!"

Peace settled again into the bakery, with the addition of slurping and sucking sounds from time to time from Manny's straw. Maria and Tomas allowed themselves to relax. Maybe this would turn out all right after all.

CHAPTER SIX

The last possible dregs of the malted milkshake slurped into the straw. Manny stared into his drink. He used his fingers to swirl the straw into the remaining bubbles, then brought the straw to his mouth to lick the final drips.

Maria and Tomas braced. Now what? It had been a nice outing so far, but how would they get their son out of the bakery without a scene. The place was filling up with people.

Manny looked around the place. His gaze didn't linger on the other customers, but flitted from object to object. His head turned faster as he took in the bustle and confusion around him. He began to rock. A low sound started in his throat and his hands rose from his sides to wave in the air.

Tomas and Maria froze, knowing what was coming, but helpless to stop it in this room full of strangers. Manny's low keening rose in pitch and volume becoming audible to everyone in the room.

Mel appeared at their table, kneeling on the floor beside Manny. She put a device on the table in front of him and rubbed her finger over the glass surface. The picture of the bakery that appeared snagged Manny's attention. Although he continued to rock, the noises stopped.

Quietly she spoke. "See, this is the bakery. You're at a table just like this one. Here's the way it goes." She looked up at Maria and smiled, then touched the right side of the screen. A view from the door appeared. "You come in the bakery. Then you walk up to the counter. You place your order." With each sentence, another picture showed on the screen, illustrating her words. "Then you sit at your table. Someone brings you something to eat or something to drink. You sit quietly and eat nicely.

Then, when you are all finished, it's time to go. You get off your chair and walk out the door with your mom or dad. You can wave good-bye to Ellie. You will come back another time."

Manny watched the whole thing intently. By the time it was over, the rocking had ceased. The screen went blank and Manny got down from his chair. He held out his hand to his dad, and then walked to the door. Outside, he stood beside his astonished father, while his mama talked to the woman, the woman who had saved them.

Maria asked her, "What did you do?"

"Sorry. Are you upset with me for interfering?" asked Mel.

"Oh, no. We are grateful. We had no idea how we were going to get our son out of the bakery without a big ruckus." Then, Maria thought about what she'd said. "I mean, our Manny, he's a good boy, but sometimes he gets upset when things don't go the way he thinks they should."

"I understand."

"You do? I'm not sure. You see, our Manny is different. I noticed your little boy. Manny is not like him." The sadness was clear in her voice.

"I'm not so sure that our boys are that different. We have our challenges with Kyle as well."

Maria forced a smile. "Kids will be kids." She held out her hand. "Thank you for your help."

"Wait! Don't you want to know what I showed your boy?"

"Si. I noticed pictures on your computer and he paid attention to them."

"That's called a social story. A woman named Carol Gray came up with the idea and it really works. I made that one for our son. He used to have trouble transitioning from one thing to another. If he liked something, he never wanted it to end. And, he really likes this bakery. So, we made a story for him. We'd read it before we'd come to the bakery and again when we got here. Then, I'd pull it out just before we were ready to leave. It worked and he got better. We don't need to use that particular one any more, but it's reassuring to have it just in case."

"We don't have a fancy computer at our house, but thank you for using yours with us."

"You don't need a computer, fancy or otherwise. You can write out a story on a piece of paper," Mel explained.

"Our Manny, he does not read."

"But he looks at pictures, I noticed. You don't need words to write a story. You can draw stick figures to illustrate what's going to happen. Just tell him what the figures mean and what is expected of him."

Maria looked skeptical that something so simple sounding could make any difference.

Mel tried to explain. "Kids with autism take in things that they see easier than things that they hear. That's why a story like this helps - the child does not just listen to what we're saying but they see the visual of what is happening."

"Kids with autism? Oh, that's not our Manny."

It was Mel's turn to look skeptical. She raised one eyebrow. "Where does he go to school?"

"He is not in school. He stays home with us."

"May I ask why?"

Maria thought it was quite obvious. "He is not like other children. He gets upset and he, well, he doesn't talk."

"Yes. So?"

Maria backed up half a step. "Pardon me?"

"I understand that he does not speak and that he might get upset, but that does not mean he can't go to school."

"No. We keep ourselves to ourselves. Manny is our responsibility. We will look after him."

"But..."

"Thank you again for your help. I must go now." And Maria left to join her husband and son to finish their walk.

Maria was quiet on the way home. Tomas thought she was just tired after the emotional turmoil of the day.

After supper, Manny dug out his favorite movie, passed it to his papa and took his mother by the hand to the couch. As he settled himself, Tomas inserted the movie and started it playing. Manny waited until Tomas sat beside him, and then shifted his dad's arm so that it was around his shoulder. Manny snuggled in between his parents, holding Maria's hand, stroking it and playing with her fingers. Part way through the movie, Manny shifted so that his head was in his mom's lap and his legs sprawled across Tomas' thighs. He moved Maria's hand onto his head so that she could stroke his hair the way he liked. Soon his breathing deepened and he slept, resting contentedly in the arms of the people who loved and cared for him. For a time, his parents enjoyed the peace of normal family life and the beauty of their trusting, slumbering child.

After Tomas carried Manny to bed, Maria let loose with the thoughts that had been plaguing her since their outing that afternoon. "Do you know what that woman said to me?"

"Which woman? You mean the one who showed that story to Manny?"

"Yes. She asked me why our son was not in school. After I told her that he did not talk and that he got upset, she still asked why."

Tomas slanted his head at his wife. "She seemed like an intelligent enough woman. Why would she even think that a child like Manny could be in school? She must have misunderstood you."

"I don't think so." A few minutes later, she added, "Maybe things are different here."

They watched television for a while. When the next advertisement came on, Maria said, "It's a social story. That's what she called the pictures she showed Manny about the bakery. She said she made that for their son."

"I noticed their boy. He did not seem like our hijo."

"She called her boy Kyle. She said he used to have trouble with transitions and didn't want to leave the bakery because he liked it there. They would show him the story and he got better at leaving when they wanted him to go."

"Well, it sure helped us out today. I was in a panic about how we were going to get him out of there. All those glass tables...."

Maria hardly took in the show they were watching, her mind churning over some of the things Mel had said. "She told me that kids with autism like to look more than listen, or something like that."

"Autism?"

"That's what she said."

"Wonder why she'd say the word autism if you were talking about Manny, or about her son?"

CHAPTER SEVEN

"Dare we try it again?" It was another gorgeous fall day, with crisp air, yet the sun still held hope in its rays. It was not a day for remaining cooped up in an apartment.

"Do you mean going for a walk or to the bakery?"

Tomas grinned. "Are you up for trying both?"

So far, it had been a good day - a good few days, actually. There had been no major upsets. Of course, there had been many smaller ones but they'd been able to head those off before any true damage was done. Maybe it helped to have both of his parents home as they could tag off with each other when one started to lose patience with their son's demands.

The walk to the bakery was a tad more challenging this week as more and more leaves littered the walkways. But, Tomas and Maria were diligent; they knew what would happen if they scrunched just one too many times. Manny remained a step ahead; he knew the route.

At the bakery, he again plastered his hands all over the glass. Maria murmured that the next time, she'd bring a cloth and cleaner and wipe her son's handprints off the glass. They gave Manny ample looking time, before holding open the door.

"Now remember son, you have to be good. Be quiet and treat the things in here gently. And, no running..." Tomas spoke to the air. Manny was already inside, scrunching down in front of the display counter.

"Well, look who's here." Ellie came around the counter to greet them. "Give me five, man." She held up her hand expectantly to Manny. He turned from the goodies, regarding her with solemn eyes. "Don't you know how to give five?" She waited. "Here," she said, grabbing for Manny's forearm.

There was an intake of breath from Maria. Tomas leaned forward, ready to intervene before his son could hurt this friendly, naive woman. Manny did *not* like to be touched, especially when he wasn't expecting it.

"Like this," Ellie continued. "See?" She raised Manny's palm to meet hers in a gentle slap. "Now, try it again." She raised her palm, holding it there expectantly. Manny did not move. Ellie raised one finger in the air and said, "Hold that thought."

"Kyle, buddy," she called. "Get over here. I need your help for a demonstration." When her nephew jogged over, she said to him, "Give me five."

With a grin, Kyle gave her hand an exuberant slap. Then he turned to the rest of the group. "Anyone else?" he asked with a raised palm.

"Sure, I'll do it," said Tomas. They slapped hands.

"And, me," said Maria. Gently, she met Kyle's hand.

Kyle turned to Manny with his hand raised. "Give me five," he said.

Manny lifted his hand to meet Kyle's. The touch was fleeting, but it happened.

Ellie looked over at her brother and sister-in-law and winked. Mel gave her a thumbs up.

Maria and Tomas stared at each other and at their son. What had just happened here?

Kyle gave a "See ya," and returned to his gingerbread cookie.

Ellie helped Manny make his choice then served him his gingerbread cookie. As they sipped their warm, fragrant drinks, Tomas and Maria commented on the way Ellie hustled around. While chatting non-stop to customers, she flew between tables, loading used dishes into a plastic tub, taking payments at the till and placing orders. Her pace made Maria uneasy. When Ellie paused to see if they wanted anything more, Tomas commented on how busy she seemed.

"I'm short-staffed. Sal's off with sick kids, so I'm bussing tables as well as the rest. Sal has five kids and they get this flu one after the other, so it looks like she'll be gone for a while. Oh well, it's not forever." Then, with a smile, she was off.

Maria watched a bit longer, then stood. "I can't stand it any longer," she told her husband. "I'm going to give her a hand. I'm just sitting here when I could at least be clearing tables for her. She's been good to Manny."

It took a while before Ellie noticed Maria quietly working away. She did notice though that she didn't need to run quite as much. Then Maria was beside her. "Where can I wash these dishes?" she asked.

"Oh, you don't' need to do that. Thank you so much for bussing tables though. Here, I'll take that." she reached for the tub of dirty dishes.

"No, I don't mind. You've been good to my Manny and he likes it here. I can help you."

"Well, if you're sure. I can definitely use the help. The dishwasher's through here."

Maria didn't notice the passage of time. It was good to feel useful and the hustle and bustle of the bakery was exciting. She felt like she was contributing and part of the team.

Carrying the dishes into the kitchen, Maria stopped short when she spied a man working at the counter. Walking with a full tub of clattering dishes, she had not entered the room silently, but he showed no sign that he sensed her presence. He gave off such an aura of concentration that she was hesitant to interrupt him. The man neither turned nor spoke. Maria hesitated, unsure if she should intrude. As she turned to back out of the room, his voice startled her.

"Well, are you going to stand there all day holding that tub?" he asked, without looking at her.

"Um, no. Ah, Ellie said the dishwasher was in here."

The man pointed to his left at the stainless steel door built into the lower cupboard. When Maria still didn't move, he looked over his shoulder at her. With no expression on his face, he returned to the dough he was punching.

Maria waited a few moments more then eased out of the room. She saw Ellie polishing the glass of the display cabinet. "Ellie," she said. "There's a man in the kitchen."

"Oh, yeah. That's Jeff, Mel's brother. He's our main cook here. Could you smell the sauerbraten he's had roasting all day?"

Sauerbraten? "Um, he looks pretty intent on what he's doing and I didn't want to disturb him."

Ellie straightened. "That's Jeff doing his thing. When he cooks, he gets into the zone and blocks out everything else. Come on. I'll introduce you."

When Maria hesitated, Ellie linked arms with her and strode towards the kitchen.

"Jeff," she called. No response. "Jeff," she said a little louder. "Turn around a minute, please."

Jeff turned, or half-turned, his hands buried in dough.

"Jeff, I'd like you to meet Maria. She's helping us out here today. Maria, this is Jeff."

Jeff held out his sticky, dough *encrusted* hand for Maria to shake.

When Maria hesitated, he asked, "Do you have problems with social skills? Did anyone teach you that you're supposed to shake hands when you're introduced to someone?"

Maria attempted to shuffle the tub of dirty dishes so that she could get a hand free.

"Nope, not this time, Jeff," said Ellie. There are exceptions to that rule and when your hands are full of streusel dough is one of the exceptions."

Jeff shrugged. "Well, suit yourself." Then he turned back to his work.

Maria's glance at Ellie questioned if she was expected to remain in the same room as this man.

"Dishwasher's right over there." Ellie pointed.

Over his shoulder, Jeff said, "I already showed her where it was."

With a squeeze of Maria's shoulder and a hasty, "Thanks", Ellie returned to the front of the bakery.

Tentatively, Maria approached the counter and set down her load. Casting glances at Jeff, she inspected the dishwasher then began the loading process. She tried to handle the crockery without any clanking so as not to disturb Jeff's concentration. Eventually she gave up on stealth when she noticed that it didn't matter anyway. Jeff's focus was intent and he seemed able to ignore her presence. She found it spooky, although not unlike being home with Manny sometimes. He, too, could concentrate so hard on what he was doing that he paid no heed to his mama, no matter what she said or did. Actually, once she got past the worry that she needed to make polite conversation to this strange man, it was soothing to be able to work in silence with her own thoughts.

When she returned to the dining room for another load of soiled dishes, Ellie explained that Jeff mainly stayed back in the kitchen, cooking. He'd occasionally step out front, especially if one of the computers was down and his skills were needed to get it operational again. But, he said he preferred to make his own chaos and liked the freedom to create food without the bother of other people.

Meanwhile, Manny was getting restless. His gingerbread man was devoured and the last slurps of his malted milkshake were history. Tomas was surprised things had remained calm for this long. When was the last time he'd been able to enjoy two peaceful cups of coffee in a row. He'd thought he was pushing his luck when he accepted a refill from Ellie, but Manny had been content.

Now, Manny's right and left legs alternately came up and toed the underside of the glass table. Tomas placed his elbows on either side of his cup to weigh the glass top down, just in case. Then, Manny started rocking - gently at first then harder as two of his chair legs left the floor at a time.

Tomas swiveled his head around the room. Where was Maria? They could not stay here much longer. And, would they be able to leave as easily as they did yesterday?

No Maria still, but instead, Ellie came by. "It's getting close to dinner time," she said. "Would Manny like to come see the options?"

Tomas quickly shook his head. Although their budget might allow them to splurge on coffee for he and Maria and a milkshake for Manny, eating supper out would take far too much of their cash. "No, thanks. We really should be going."

"I'd really like you to stay and have supper with me. My treat. I don't know how else to repay Maria for helping out here. I already offered to pay her for her time, but she declined."

"You were good to us and to our Manny, so Maria wanted to give a hand. She saw how hard you were working. She's good at these things is my Maria. In the village where we are from, people help each other."

"Well, she saved my life this afternoon all right. Now please, let me serve you a meal. I guarantee it will be delicious. Jeff is a skilled chef." She held out her hand to Manny. "Come. I'll show you your choices."

Before Tomas could formulate a polite refusal, Manny had jumped down from his chair, taken Ellie's hand and was standing on a stool to see the top of the counter. Ellie kept one steadying hand on his shoulder and one at the small of his back. And, Manny let her.

Soon he returned, walking oh so carefully heel to toe, both hands tightly strangling a china plate, balancing steaming sauerbraten on a fresh ciabatta bun with a side of mixed green salad. Behind him came Ellie with two identical plates. With a flourish, she set the two on their table and rescued the third from Manny's hands. "Your son chose the meal for you. He wanted all of you to have the same thing." Turning to look at his son, she said, "Oh, we forgot the cutlery. Do you remember where they are?" Without answering, Manny took off for the counter where three sets of utensils were wrapped snuggly in cloth napkins.

Tomas rose from his chair. "We don't let Manny handle knives or forks. They're too sharp."

"Looks like he's managing this time." And, sure enough, he did. "I'll go round up Maria to join you. And, thanks for loaning her to me. I can't tell you how much her help meant today. You know, if she ever has some spare time and wants a job, we'll take her. Any hours she could give us would be welcomed."

Maria flushed as she took her seat, head down and beaming at the praise. "It was nothing. I enjoyed it."

Tomas did not look as pleased. "Maria has all she can do being a wife and mother to us. We don't leave her much free time on her hands. We need her at home."

Tomas was up early, consuming too strong, too hot coffee and perusing the help wanted section of the paper. The pickings were pitiful. The last three warehouse jobs he'd called said they only took applications in person and to come over and get in line. He'd done just that. For one, the highest paying job, the line of hopefuls snaked outside the building and around the corner. That was over a hundred guys vying for two openings. Nonetheless, Tomas had waited, shuffling ahead a few steps every ten minutes or so. When he worked his way up to the building's entrance, the shout passed down the line, "Position's filled. Head on home the rest of you."

The next two he tried for didn't have quite as much competition, but he had no luck with either. There were guys with more experience who got the jobs.

Today, Tomas' plan was to find the best possibility and be there long before the doors even opened so he'd be first in line. But the choices in the paper were meager.

Maria was so hopeful for him. She just knew that a fine man like Tomas would find a grand job; anyone could see what a good worker he'd be. Although she said all the right things and smiled for him at the right times, he had caught her counting the money in the sugar bowl when she thought he wasn't looking.

What kind of a man would let his wife worry like that? What kind of a man did not look after his family?

But today, today would be different. It had to be.

And, it was different. The position at the janitorial supply warehouse did not have a line-up of would-be employees. Tomas was pleased that he seemed to be the first person there. Mr. Blakely interviewed him, then said that they had never given a man a job without first trying him out. That gave them a chance to see what they think of Tomas and Tomas time to see if this was the kind of place he'd like to work. They considered this time as training, sort of a non-paying apprenticeship. Tomas wouldn't mind working for a day on a volunteer basis, so they could get an idea of just what kind of worker he was, would he? Look at it as an investment in his future, in a company where there was room to grow.

Certainly, Tomas wouldn't mind, especially when they said it might be just for the morning.

So, he moved crates, unpacked boxes and shelved items. When a truck drove in for a load of certain cleaning supplies, Tomas loaded the cartons. It was warm in the warehouse, without the type of ventilation Tomas had been used to at Mr. Humber's shop. But, despite the sweat streaking down his face and the way his shirt clung to his aching muscles, Tomas did his best to demonstrate his worthiness.

Lunch time came and went. No one came near Tomas to check on his work or see how he was doing. No one told him where the break room was or what hours he'd have free for lunch. So, Tomas worked on. And on.

Finally, at four-thirty, Tomas noticed some of the lights in the office out front going out. Then the warehouse lights dimmed. He waited a few minutes, but none came back on. In fact, the hallway lights turned off. Quietly, Tomas walked in that direction, searching for Mr. Blakely or anyone to tell him what was going on. The front offices were dim with only the setting sun's light from the grimy outside windows. He did not see a soul. Hesitating, he climbed the stairs to the office where he'd been interviewed so many hours ago. Timidly, he knocked on the closed door. A muffled, "Yeah" sounded.

Tomas turned the knob and poked just his head through. "Excuse me, Mr. Blakely," he said. "I wondered what hours I should be keeping. The lights went out and I don't see anyone else around."

"Well, Tomas, is it? Around here we're not partial to clock watchers. This is generally quitting time, as long as the work is done. Did you finish putting away all the load that came in on that semi-trailer?"

"Almost all of it, sir."

"So, you're telling me the job's not done yet?"

"Not quite. I worked non-stop sir, as quickly as I could."

"Hmmm." Blakely frowned and waited.

"But, I can finish up before I leave today."

"Good, good. That will be good." He returned to his paperwork.

"Excuse me, but should I return tomorrow? Did you find my work satisfactory during this training?"

"Let's say that the verdict is still out. How be we give it another try tomorrow and see what we think of each other?"

"All right. I'll just finish up that load then be here early tomorrow morning."

It had been dark when Tomas reached home the day before. All that physical work, plus not eating all day left him famished. He was never so grateful to tuck into a plate of Maria's tamales. He was tired, but confident that he'd found a job. He explained to Maria about the temporary volunteering that would soon turn into a permanent job, one with room for advancement.

The next day he left home even earlier, determined to make a good impression. When he arrived, the doors were locked. Almost fifty minutes later, Mr. Blakely arrived and slapped Tomas on the back. "Good to see an eager worker," he said, ushering Tomas back toward the warehouse. "I see you brought your lunch today. That's the sign of a man prepared to work."

Today progressed much as had the day before, but this time with two semi-trucks unloading and even more boxes to be stored away, all the while filling orders for arriving pickup trucks. If this was a fall day and it was this hot in the warehouse, Tomas wondered fleetingly what it would be like in the summer? Still, he worked as if his life depended on it. Periodically he'd glance around, expecting to see an observer or even partially hidden cameras so someone could check on the quality of his work. Certainly, no one came into the warehouse to watch him. Just as he'd think he had made it through the list of tasks, he'd notice another one tacked to the hanging clip board.

Tomas put even more effort into the job today than the day before. This would be his last trial day. Tonight, he and Maria would celebrate his new job.

When the lights turned off this time, Tomas inspected the tidy warehouse one last time and was satisfied with the job he'd done. He climbed the stairs to knock on the door to Mr. Blakely's office. "Excuse me, sir," he said. "I've finished for the day. Are there some papers you would like me to sign to get onto the payroll?"

"I was meaning to come down and talk to you about that today, but as you can see, this mound of paper has kept me at it all day."

Tomas waited expectantly.

"It looks like you picked up your pace a trifle today."

"Yes, sir."

"We're still not sure you have what it takes to make it in our organization. Our standards are high."

Tomas frowned.

"Let's say we give it one more day, and then we'll have a deal. Shake on it?"

Tomas hesitated then came forward and shook the man's hand.

"So, we'll see you then tomorrow morning?"

Tomas nodded.

"You know, I think you just might make it here."

With those encouraging words, Tomas walked home with a lighter heart. Tomorrow. Just one more day, then he'd have a job and be able to provide once more for his family. What was two days' work for free compared to a permanent position and room for advancement?

"Maria, let's celebrate. After supper we'll head to the bakery for a treat."

"Do you think we should? You haven't been paid yet, and we've never taken Manny there in the evening."

"Querida, you worry too much. I have proven my worth as a worker to Mr. Blakely. What would his warehouse look like without me? He has no one else to do the job."

"But, Manny..."

"Manny's been an angel in that bakery every single time. He likes it there."

"And, they like him."

"Yes, they do seem to like our son. Let's go."

It was dusk as they donned their jackets. Manny was fine until they reached the outside door of the apartment and he saw that it was no longer bright daylight. Manny only left the house during the day. He balked, not responding to their, "Come on son", or the pull of his hand. His shoulders reached for his ears, one hand rose to his side and the other fingers entered his mouth. A low, keening sound began. Tomas' voice rose as he sternly ordered his son outside.

"Wait," said Maria. "Let me try something." She rummaged in her purse until she found a scrap of paper and a pen. "Manny, we're going to the bakery. See?" She drew a sketch of three stick figures walking - one smaller, holding the hands of the two larger figures on either side of him. "This is you, me and papa walking down the sidewalk to the bakery." Then she drew the same stick figures sitting at a small table. "We'll have a snack there and something to drink and then come home."

Manny's flapping hand stilled and he used it to hold the paper with his mother. When he stared intently at the drawings, Maria recited the whole story again, and then waited. It took seconds, seconds in which Maria feared that her son was mulling it over, trying to decide whether or not to comply, and then he stepped through the door his father was holding and waited.

Now what, thought Maria? Manny remained in that fixed position, hands out to either side, staring straight ahead. "What? What is it, Manny?" Part of her wondered why she even asked. Never, not even once in his whole nine years had Manny ever given her a response. She walked in front of her son and turned to look at him.

Manny turned his face toward her and held out his hand. She took it. He remained fixed with his other empty hand stuck out. His dad stepped forward and took that outstretched hand. As soon as Tomas completed his grasp, Manny's footsteps started down the sidewalk toward the bakery, leaving his parents staring at each other over his head. "It worked!" mouthed Maria.

Indeed, it did and the visit went smoothly. Ellie was still on duty, which made Maria wonder at the hours she kept. As always, Ellie dropped what she was doing to high-five Manny, and then inspect the display case with him. Despite the array of goodies, Manny always chose the same thing.

But tonight, with the job prospect securely in his pocket, Tomas wanted to splurge on a treat for himself and his wife as well. Maria chose a cream puff bulging with piped whipping cream and topped with snowy confectioners' sugar. Tomas had a gooey chocolate éclair.

Without many customers in the bakery, Ellie pulled up a chair to join them.

"This pastry is muy fantastico," Maria told her.

"Thanks. I make them myself. And how's yours?" She turned to Tomas.

"Heavenly. I feel like a kid who wants to lick his fingers."

"Have at it. I certainly do," Ellie said.

Maria asked, "Aren't you going to have one?"

Ellie waved her hand. "No. Definitely not. Do you have any idea how many of those I've consumed in my life? Or how I so do not enjoy them anymore after baking them every day? They're favorites with my customers, but to be honest, I'm sick of them."

"You should taste some of my wife's churros," said Tomas. "There are none better."

"Churros? I'm not sure I've ever had one of those."

"They're a piped, fried dough laced with anise and vanilla and sprinkled with cinnamon and sugar," explained Maria. "They are common where we come from."

"Do you have any? I wouldn't mind tasting one some time."

"The next time I make a batch, we will bring you some."

Ellie paused a minute, then turned to look at both Tomas and Maria. Then, she addressed Maria. "You know, variety is good and it's nice to change it up. This bakery was floundering before Jeff came on board. He brought in new ideas and new dishes. Now, our food menu changes daily, but our pastries remain about the same.

"Do you think you might ever consider making some churros that I could sell here? I could front you the initial ingredients, then you could work out what you'd need for your time and labor."

Tomas had stiffened. "My wife cooks for our family and sometimes for our friends. She has her hands full looking after her family."

"Tomas, this I could do at home. It would not take away from the time I give to you and to Manny. I like baking, you know that. But we can only eat so much, the three of us." Her eyes pleaded with her husband, trying to see past his stern look. "Why don't we try just one batch? I could make it and you bring it to Ellie to see what she thinks."

"We'll see," was his reply.

Maria gave Ellie a tentative smile.

"Well, I'd sure appreciate it if you could see your way through to help me out," replied Ellie, catching Maria's eye.

CHAPTER EIGHT

Confident that he now had the job, Tomas did not set his alarm clock any earlier than he had the day before. Still, he was again the first person to arrive at the warehouse. He pulled the collar of his jacket up against the damp, morning air as he waited, shifting from foot to foot. At the loading dock sat a semi-truck and an impatient driver. Tomas could do nothing but apologize to the trucker; he had no keys to raise the door to help the guy unload.

Mr. Blakely approached on the sidewalk, with his shoulders hunched, eyes on the ground. He jerked his head up at Tomas' greeting, as if startled to see him there. Preoccupied, thought Tomas.

With a nod, Blakely said, "Looks like it's time to get at 'er for another day." He unlocked the door, and then headed up the stairs to his office. Tomas watched his retreating back for a few seconds then headed to the warehouse to fire up the fork lift.

It was a few minutes before one o'clock when Tomas entered the break room to grab a bite of lunch. He stood, his mouth full of sandwich when Mr. Blakely entered, accompanied by another man, of about his age.

"Good to see that you're almost finished your lunch, Tomas. You can pack up your things and be on your way. Your replacement is here now. Wish things could have worked out better."

Tomas' eyebrows lifted and he stared. The new guy didn't meet his eyes. Blakely only held his gaze fleetingly. "You heard me," he said. "Go on, get out of here now. Better luck at your next job."

"Next job? I thought I had this one. Mr. Blakely, this is my third day working for you and I have done everything you asked of me. I know I've done a good job."

"That might be your opinion but I disagree and I'm the boss."

"But you said that the first day was training to see how we liked each other then you told me to come back. I did." He pointed down the hall. "Go look at the warehouse. I bet it's never been in better shape."

Now Mr. Blakely faced him. "Don't make this any harder on anyone than it has to be. Surely this is not the first job you've been sacked from. Now, go on. Get out. Guys like you are a dime a dozen."

Tomas drew himself up and faced his former employer directly. "I see. I'll go as soon as I get my pay."

"Pay, what pay? You were here as a volunteer trainee and it didn't work out. Get off my premises."

The other gentleman had stood in the background, trying to be invisible. Now, he and Tomas exchanged glances. To Tomas he asked, "Did you agree to volunteer for a day as a trainee?"

"Yes. That was the arrangement."

"And what happened after that?"

"This man," and Tomas pointed at Mr. Blakely, "told me he was unsure of my work and to come back the next day. I worked my butt off, sweat pouring off me all day in that stuffy warehouse and I didn't stop once for a break. I stayed late and finished every item on the task list. And, that was just the first day. The next day I arrived an hour earlier, before the doors were even opened and did the same thing. No one came back to help or to check on me."

The new guy turned to Mr. Blakely. "Is that right? Is that what you plan for my volunteer training day? And the next?"

The guy pivoted to face Tomas. "Hi. I'm Paul." He stuck out his hand. "I've heard of scams like this. Employers too cheap to hire help run these ads to get free labor. Then, before the guy wises up to what's going on, he gets 'fired' and another newbie shows up to do the sweat labor."

"Can they do that?" asked Tomas.

"Not legally. And not morally, but guys like this have no ethics." He took two steps towards the door. "Hey," he said to Tomas. "Can I buy you a coffee?"

"Wait!" said Blakely. You're not leaving, are you? We had a deal. You're starting work for me today."

"As if I'd work for a scum bag like you."

"But who's going to unload the trucks?" Blakely hollered.

Tomas looked over his shoulder and pointed at Blakely. Paul didn't bother turning his head, but gave him the finger over his shoulder. "I know of this coffee shop," he told Tomas. "It's not that far and the food is worth the walk."

Soon, Tomas realized just where his new acquaintance was taking him for coffee. "Do you know Ellie?" he asked.

"Yeah. She went to school with my little sister and I played football with her brother, Ben. Madson's not that big of a place and this bakery has been in their family since I was a kid."

Paul and Tomas walked directly to the counter to place their orders, intent on their conversation. Not until he turned around to find a table did Tomas really look around. His eyes lighted on his family. Maria and Manny shared a small table, Manny intent on dismantling his gingerbread man, Maria reading a book.

Just then Manny raised his head and spied his father. His eyes got large, his mouth opened and a word came out. Just one word, but oh, such a word. One he'd never uttered before. "Papa!"

Maria's head came up. She stared at her son. Did that word come out of his mouth? "What? What, Manny?"

"Papa." He didn't blink. His eyes never left his father's face.

Tomas was frozen. Had his son spoken? Had he said what he thought he'd heard?

Maria turned to follow Manny's gaze and saw her husband staring agape at their son.

"Say it. Say it again," Maria instructed Manny.

Manny began rocking and his attention returned to his cookie.

Tomas slowly approached on wooden legs, his eyes full of wonder. "Maria! Did you hear? Did my Manny call me Papa?"

"I, I think so. He said it twice even. Oh, Tomas!" She leapt up and threw her arms around Tomas's neck, sloshing his coffee onto them both. "Oh, sorry. I'll get a cloth." And, she was gone, leaving Tomas regarding their son with such pride.

He ruffled Manny's hair and gave him a hug. "How is my little man?" This was the typical greeting he gave, never expecting nor ever receiving a response. This time, though, he waited, afraid that if he even moved, the spell would be broken and Manny would retreat to silence. He waited and waited some more. The gingerbread man seemed to hold more interest for Manny than did his father's presence. The moment seemed gone, but both he and Maria had heard that one special word, so it must be true.

Tomas looked around the room to see if anyone else was in awe of the miracle. One person watched and celebrated with him. Mel, the woman who had drawn them that story observed the incident. She knew just what this meant for the parents and more importantly, for Manny. She grinned and gave Tomas a thumbs up. Then, while she held his attention, she pointed to herself, moved her tips of her fingers across the table in a walking motion and then held up her index finger. Tomas nodded his head like a bobble doll.

Maria was back with paper napkins, wiping off her husband and the table, bubbling over with excitement. "He did it! He really did. Manny spoke. Oh, Tomas do you know what this means? Maybe he'll do it more and more. Maybe..."

Tomas hugged her to him and kissed the top of her head. Then he remembered where they were. He'd forgotten himself. He and Maria did not show affection in public; that was for private times. He turned and noticed Paul waiting behind him, blowing on the foam and sipping this latte.

Ellie came by with their pastries and greeted Paul with a kiss on his cheek. "How's it going? How many rug rats do you and Sue have now?"

Paul gave her shoulders a squeeze with his free hand. "Just two and most days they are more than we can handle."

Maria followed this quizzically. And, why was Tomas even here? He was supposed to be at his new job.

"Paul, I'd like you to meet my wife, Maria and my son, Manny." They nodded and smiled at each other. "Let's sit down." He pulled over an empty table to join theirs. "Maria, I have some bad news." He and Paul related the scam that Tomas had fallen into.

Cleaning tables around them, Ellie piped in. "I've heard about that, too."

Jeff's hand was deep in the innards of a computer along the back wall. "The United States Supreme Court in Walling v. Portland Terminal Co. serves as a landmark case on employer treatment of trainees," he informed them. He continued in their silence. "They call it the Walling Factors, the criteria used to determine if a trainee or intern should be paid." Jeff looked up at the group. "You know all this, don't you?"

All four adults shook their heads side to side.

"Basically, if the trainee is gaining the same skills or experience he would at a vocational institute, he can go unpaid because he's not an employee. The training must be for the benefit of the trainee and the trainee can't be taking the job of someone who should be paid for that work."

When his audience continued to stare, he tried to explain more fully. "Look, it's simple. If the training is mainly for the benefit of the trainee, he does not have to get paid. If the work done is mainly for the benefit of the employer, then the trainee needs to be paid. Look it up in the Department of Labor website." Jeff returned to beefing up the RAM in the aging computer.

"What kind of job are you looking for?" Tomas asked Paul.

"I used to be a realtor, but you know what's happened to that business since the recession. The company I worked for folded. I'm good with my hands and have a strong back, so I'll try just about anything."

"That's about where I'm at, too," Tomas said.

"Why don't we help each other out? Most places are looking to hire more than one guy." He walked a few steps over to nab a discarded newspaper. Thumbing through until he found the classified section, he gave half to Tomas. "Why don't we both look and let the other know when we see something promising. Here." He scrawled his phone number on a napkin and passed it to Tomas. Tomas did the same for him.

They sat back to enjoy their fragrant brews, and eat churros. Churros? Tomas looked at the warm, sweet and spicy cinnamon treat. These tasted just like the churros Maria made.

Maria sat there beaming at him. She nodded. "Yes, I made a batch so Ellie could see what churros are. She ate one, then two and asked if she can serve them to her customers. And, look," she gestured around the room. "Some people even went back for seconds."

"*You* made these?" Paul asked. "My compliments to the chef. Tomas, you're one lucky man."

They watched Ellie fly around the room; it was hard to miss her non-stop motion. There were customers standing by the door, waiting for a clean table. Others entered the bakery, but upon seeing a line-up, retreated and walked up the street. The strain on Ellie was obvious.

Maria stood. "Tomas, I have to help her. Will you stay here with Manny for a few minutes?"

"With a boy who calls me Papa? Anytime."

Paul finished his coffee and left for home. He had to meet his kids after school; his wife was working late that week.

Tomas had downed the last of his coffee and finished off Maria's, too. Manny had nothing left to eat or drink and was tiring of playing with his fingers. Tomas glanced around for Maria, who was nowhere to be found.

Ellie noticed him searching and stopped by to explain that his wife was in the kitchen helping put together the calzones for the supper crowd. She searched his face then made a decision. "Tomas, I'm really strapped here as you can see. With Sally out there is just too much work here for Jeff and me to keep up. I have another worker coming in at six o'clock, but until then, do you think there's any chance that Maria could stay and give us a hand? I can't tell you how grateful I'd be. She's such a help and I'm desperate. As you can see, I'm losing customers when I can't keep up and I can't afford to turn away business."

"What does Maria say?"

As he said the words, his wife appeared behind Ellie. "Please, Tomas, I'd like to stay and help Ellie if you think you could handle Manny on your own this afternoon." Her black eyes pleaded with him.

"Is this what you want?"

Maria nodded, her eyes not leaving his.

"You are helping out a friend?"

Again, Maria nodded.

Even a stranger could read the misgivings on Tomas's face. But, it was hard to refuse Maria anything she wanted and she asked for so little.

Reluctantly he gave one nod.

The smile Maria returned made it worth it. He'd do just about anything to have her beam at him that way.

"Please come back and have supper here. It's the least I can do," said Ellie.

Manny, meantime, had lost patience with all the adult talk. He'd sat long enough and roughly pushed his chair away from the table. From long experience, Tomas' and Maria's hands were there to catch the table, just in case. Manny walked to the door. When only his dad followed, he scanned the room for his mother. Tomas opened the door and took Manny's hand. Manny's feet were rooted to the floor.

"Come on, son. Mama's staying here. We'll come back for her later, after we go for a walk and play a bit."

Manny rose to his toes and sucked in a deep breath.

Oh, no, thought Maria. It's going to happen. He's been so good and now they'll never want us back in the bakery again.

The keening sound rose to a shriek. The flapping hands knocked against the closed, glass door.

Then, Mel approached. In her hand was the iPad she'd been working on. "May I?" she asked Tomas, raising her voice to be heard above Manny's wails.

Ashamed to admit he needed a stranger's help managing his son, but remembering the magic she'd worked the last time, he said, "Please. If you can help, go ahead."

Mel knelt on the floor beside Manny, dodging out of the way of his waving arms. She set her iPad on her lap and placed a hand on each of Manny's shoulders. Tomas could see that she was pressing down hard. Harder than he thought she should for a little boy. He was stepping forward to intervene when she spoke to his son.

"See Manny? Here's the story we read last time about the bakery." And she read it to him again. Gradually, the shrieks decreased, the flapping slowed and he came down off his toes. His attention focused on the pictures of the bakery on the iPad. "See? There's you sitting at the table. And there's your mom and your dad. Now, it's time to go.

"But it's different this time. We're changing it a bit. This time, Manny and Papa are going home for a little while. Mama has to stay here and help Ellie. See? Here they are working in the picture. And, here is Manny and Papa going out the door to walk home. In a little while, you and Papa will come back here to get Mama. You'll eat supper together, and then all of you will go home." Her voice dropped on the last words with a tone of finality.

She stood. "See you later." Then she turned her back and walked back to her table. She stopped once to wave.

Manny responded to the tug of his father's hand and left the bakery to the words of Tomas. "We'll go home and play with your blocks, then later we'll come back to get Mama. Won't that be fun? You get to go to the bakery twice in one day." Tomas prayed that his words were true and the afternoon would be fun.

CHAPTER NINE

Mel came over to where Maria and Ellie were standing. The tension had not yet left Maria's shoulders but she gave Mel a weak smile.

"Thanks," she said. "Thank you very much. That could have been so much worse. You could not imagine what Manny can be like when he gets going."

"Oh, I have a fair idea," Mel told her with a grin. "I'm in a profession where I can say I've almost seen it all, at least where kids are concerned."

"You're a nurse?"

"No, I'm a teacher."

"She teaches kids with special needs," Ellie explained. "Her specialty is kids with autism."

"I am sure you have never seen a boy like our Manny. He can be a handful." She thought a minute. "Does that always work? I mean that story thing on your iPad?"

"Well, is there anything that works every time with all kids? No, it doesn't work as often as I'd like, but yeah, it often does work. Some kids with autism have a difficult time making sense of the words they hear. If you show them what you want them to know, it can make it easier for them to understand. Some of the unwanted behaviors are because the child is anxious and not sure what's coming next or what will be expected of him. Transitions are especially hard for them and a story like this can help."

"We don't have an iPad."

"Doesn't matter. Paper will do just fine."

"I'm not sure why it helped Manny, because he doesn't have autism; I've heard about autism and Manny's not like that. But I'm glad your story worked this time. Thank you again for helping us. You were so kind." With a smile and nod at Mel, Maria picked up the nearby tub and began clearing tables.

Ellie asked Mel, "Why does she say that Manny doesn't have autism?"

"I saw what happened out there," Jeff told Maria when she came into the kitchen to load the dishwasher. "You should let Mel help you."

"We did. Her story helped Tomas get Manny out of the bakery without a fuss. Or, at least without much of one."

"My sister knows what she's doing. She's really good with kids who have autism."

"Why does everyone assume Manny has autism? My son is not autistic!" Despite her defiant words, Jeff was unruffled.

He continued, "If you want to say so," and turned his attention back to his mixing bowl. A minute passed, and then he thought better of it, but spoke with his back to Maria. "Why do you say he doesn't? It's plain to everyone else that that kid has autism. What do you think it is that makes him different?"

"I have heard of autism. Those kids are far, far worse than our Manny. They are in their own world. They just rock and bang their heads. Some never talk. They are hopeless. That is not my son."

"Hmm. I think I've seen Manny rock. Does he ever bang his head? And, I haven't exactly noticed him chatting up a storm when he's here. But maybe he saves all his chatter for when he's home. Right?"

Maria could honestly say one thing. "He spoke. Right here in this bakery. He said 'Papa'".

"That's great. It's encouraging. But is that normal for someone his age? You and Tomas acted like it was a big deal, not something that happens every day. I'm not good at reading facial expressions, but I'd say that both of you guys looked shocked."

Maria looked down but had to be honest. Her voice low, she said, "That was the first word he has ever said." Fists gripping both side of the tub, she stared at the assortment of dirty utensils. "We have been terrified that he will never talk. How would he get by if he can't talk? And then, he said 'Papa'. You don't know what that meant to us."

"No," agreed Jeff. "But I might have a better idea of what it meant to Manny."

"I don't understand."

"No, you might not. It's an autism thing."

"I would be happier if you would not talk about autism. That is not Manny."

"Why are you so against your kid having autism?"

"Because then what would happen to him? Now, we have hope but if he had autism we would lose all that." Shaking her head, Maria said, "It cannot be true. What would become of him if ever he had autism?"

"Maybe he'd be a baker or a chef like me."

Ruefully, Maria shook her head. "I have tasted your cooking. That is not something someone with autism could do."

Jeff turned to look at Maria. He waited until she stopped rattling dishes and faced him. "I have autism," he informed her.

The fistful of cutlery Maria clutched clattered to the floor. She gaped at Jeff.

"You should close your mouth. That's not a good look on you," Jeff told her.

Maria's bottom teeth came up to join their partners. "What did you say?" she asked.

"You heard me. So from now on, you'd better watch what you say about autism. No slams, no stereotypes and no denying."

"Denying?"

Exasperated, Jeff placed his wrists on his hips, dangling floury hands to the side. "Just why do you think everyone keeps mentioning the word 'autism' in your presence? Or more correctly, in the presence of your son?"

"I don't know. I honestly can't figure that out. No one has ever said that before we started coming to this bakery."

"Maybe that's because we're like family here and in our family, we understand about autism. Ellie's boyfriend Rob teaches kids who have autism. My sister Mel is likely the best autism specialist you're ever going to find. Her son Kyle has autism. I have autism. Maybe that's why we talk about it and why we can spot it in someone else, too. Like your son."

Maria loaded the dishwasher in silence. Wiping her hands on her apron, she shook her head and told Jeff, "No, I don't think so."

Before Jeff could reply, she grabbed her tub and left the kitchen.

Twenty minutes later, Maria returned to the kitchen. Rather than heading straight to the dishwasher as was her habit, she perched the overflowing tub on the counter and watched Jeff baste the garlic chicken breasts. "Can I ask you some questions?"

"Don't you mean, 'may'?"

"Pardon?"

"It's 'May I ask some questions', not 'can'. Of course, you physically can, but I think you were asking for my permission. Yes."

Maria, slightly baffled by Jeff's grammar lesson, asked, "Yes?"

"Aren't you going to ask me something?"

"You say you have autism?" Her voice rose at the end of the sentence.

"We're already established that."

"But you're not like those people I've seen in movies."

"When you've met one person with autism, you've met one person with autism. Look, everyone's different, has different skills, abilities and challenges. Are you the same as every other Spanish speaking women?"

"Of course not."

"How do you think it's any different with people who have autism? Look, I have autism. It's one of my characteristics, just like one of yours is that you have dark hair. Autism does not define who I am, it's just a part of me and might affect how I think and do some things."

Maria had to mull this over, so she worked at cleaning up the countertop. "And you think this is why my Manny can't talk?"

"You'll have to ask Mel. She knows more about that kind of stuff. This is what she studied in her Master's degree."

Quietly, Maria asked, "What makes you think Manny has autism?"

"Have you seen how he rocks when he gets upset or bored? Flaps his hands? The sounds he made when he had to leave the bakery with just his dad because that was unexpected? And, what does he do every time he comes here? He spends ages looking over his choices, then picks exactly the same treat each time."

"I didn't know you were watching."

"I may hang out in the back cooking, but I see what goes on in here."

Jeff continued. "I bet he doesn't like it when you change things up. Like he always leaves the bakery with both his parents. Do you have to walk the same route to get here each time?'

"Yes, we do. You should see what happens if we try to take another way."

"Yep, I get it. Been there, done that."

"But now you change things yourself. You cook something different every day."

"I'm older now and I've learned strategies that help me. I can't say that I don't prefer things to be the same way, but I'm way more adaptable now than when I was a kid."

"Do you think Manny will become that way, too?" There was so much hope in Maria's voice.

"Depends. He'll learn some things on his own, but he'll need help."

"What kind of help?"

"The kind experienced people can give; people like Mel."

"Do you think my Manny could ever be like you?"

"Nope. Those would be pretty big shoes to fill, don't you think?" Jeff grinned at her. "Manny can find his own way and he might just surprise you."

They worked in silence, Maria washing and putting away the cooking pots Jeff had just finished with. Then, she helped him prepare the Panini sandwiches, ready for grilling for the customers' orders during the supper time rush.

Washing his hands, Jeff asked over his shoulder, "So, why isn't Manny in school?"

CHAPTER TEN

For Maria, the afternoon had flown by. This was work? Why did people grumble about having to go to work? For her, this was fun. She had not realized how much it would mean to her to get out of the house, to meet other people and to not worry intensely about Manny every second of her waking day. Several times she felt nasty twinges of guilt when it crossed her mind to wonder how Tomas was doing with Manny. He was a good dad and they'd be fine, but he was not used to being home alone with their son. Still, if Manny got violent, Tomas was better able to subdue him than was she.

The way people complimented her on her work warmed Maria's heart. This was basically the sort of housework she did at home daily, but here, well, here people appreciated it. She felt bad for letting that thought enter her mind. Of course, Tomas appreciated what a good homemaker she was, but somehow, here it was different. She was part of a team working to make the bakery a success. It was exciting and fun. Was it all right though to be enjoying herself so much when her family was at home?

The next time the bell over the door tinkled, Maria was too busy to look up. But, as she turned with a loaded tub of used dishes, a whirlwind grabbed her around the waist and squeezed. Tomas was there to catch the tub and steady his wife with one hand. Maria looked into the smiling face of her son. Manny. She grabbed him tightly and rocked back and forth with him before giving him a kiss on his disheveled head. She rubbed their noses together and he giggled. Actually giggled. Wow. This was the sweet Manny, the memories they held dear to their hearts against the times when things got tough.

If this was the kind of greeting she got after not seeing her son for a few hours, she should go out to work more often.

It was a few minutes before six o'clock. Maria was secretly just a little disappointment to see her replacement enter the bakery, wash her hands and don her apron. With a flourish, Ellie brought over three steaming plates of dinner for Maria, Tomas and Manny. She told Manny to come find her after he'd finished eating everything on his child's size plate and she'd help him pick out his treat. Manny's eyes followed her retreating back. Sensing this, Ellie turned around and pointed to his plate. "First, eat that. Then, the treat." Her tone brooked no argument. She shared a wink with Mel. "See," she mouthed to her sister-in-law, "I can learn." The first....then.... strategy was one she'd seen Mel use often with Kyle.

It worked with Manny, at least this time. Deep in conversation, his parents had not noticed that he'd cleaned his plate. What drew their attention was the rocking of the table as Manny pushed back to get down from his chair and go find Ellie. The room was small enough and his parents were now not as apprehensive about this behavior so they let him go, confident that Ellie would pay attention to Manny, as promised. Even that worked well.

Mel gathered up her used dishes and took them to the bucket on the counter. Returning, she pulled up a chair at Maria and Tomas' table and asked, "Mind if I join you for a minute?"

Maria and Tomas shuffled their chairs over to make room. Once settled, Mel took out her iPad. "Would you like me to leave this here with you in case you need to go over the story before you leave? It's getting dark outside."

Perplexed, Tomas said, "We know the way and there are streetlights."

Mel laughed. "I wasn't thinking about you. No, it's Manny here I wondered about. It's different walking home in the dark from what he's used to in the daylight. If he's only ever been here in the day, you may find that he's startled to see that it's dark outside."

She had a point. They'd never walked with their son after dark.

"Thanks, but no. We've never ran one of those things."

"I'll show you. It's simple. You press this round button at the side to turn it on. Then this bar and the words 'Slide to Unlock' appear. Take your finger and slide in the direction of the arrow." She passed it over to Tomas.

"Which finger?" he asked.

"Doesn't matter. Just not the one covered in jelly, please, although the screen's washable. Kids use these all the time."

Tomas slid the white bar and a picture of Manny in the bakery appeared. He held it up for his son to see. "See Manny? It's you."

Manny continued to crunch one leg of his gingerbread man, but watched the screen.

Mel leaned over. "Now, see this arrow in the middle of the picture? Touch it with your finger and the story will start."

Sure enough, it did. They all sat and listened and watched as the story of Manny at the bakery unfolded.

"Thank you very much. It's an amazing machine," said Maria. "Manny likes his story."

Mel stood up. "When you're done with the iPad, just leave it behind the counter. Ellie will get it to me or Ben when we're back tomorrow or the next day."

"Don't you need it tonight?"

"Nah, we're good. Keep it with you just in case you need it." She circled the table to where Manny was digging off the gingerbread man's icing eyes. "High five, buddy." She held up her hand.

Maria and Tomas watched, fearful that their son was going to be rude to this helpful woman. But Mel just crouched there patiently, her eyes not leaving Manny's face.

Tomas made to reach for Manny's arm to guide his hand to meet Mel's. Mel turned her face just a fraction towards Tomas and shook her head no.

Another few seconds passed. Manny did not look directly at Mel, but raised his hand to lightly tap hers.

Mel grinned. "Good boy." To his parents, "See you guys."

It was a few minutes before six o'clock. Maria was secretly just a little disappointed to see her replacement enter the bakery, wash her hands and don her apron. With a flourish, Ellie brought over three steaming plates of dinner for Maria, Tomas and Manny. She told Manny to come find her after he'd finished eating everything on his child's size plate and she'd help him pick out his treat. Manny's eyes followed her retreating back. Sensing this, Ellie turned around and pointed to his plate. "First, eat that. Then, the treat." Her tone brooked no argument. She shared a wink with Mel. "See," she mouthed to her sister-in-law, "I can learn." The first....then.... strategy was one she'd seen Mel use often with Kyle.

It worked with Manny, at least this time. Deep in conversation, his parents had not noticed that he'd cleaned his plate. What drew their attention was the rocking of the table as Manny pushed back to get down from his chair and go find Ellie. The room was small enough and his parents were now not as apprehensive about this behavior so they let him go, confident that Ellie would pay attention to Manny, as promised. Even that worked well.

Mel gathered up her used dishes and took them to the bucket on the counter. Returning, she pulled up a chair at Maria's and Tomas' table and asked, "Mind if I join you for a minute?"

Maria and Tomas shuffled their chairs over to make room. Once settled,

Mel took out her iPad. "Would you like me to leave this here with you in case you need to go over the story before you leave? It's getting dark outside."

Perplexed, Tomas said, "We know the way and there are streetlights."

Mel laughed. "I wasn't thinking about you. No, it's Manny here I wondered about. It's different walking home in the dark from what he's used to in the daylight. If he's only ever been here in the day, you may find that he's startled to see that it's dark outside."

She had a point. They'd never walked with their son after dark.

"Thanks, but no. We've never ran one of those things."

"I'll show you. It's simple. You press this round button at the side to turn it on. Then this bar and the words 'Slide to Unlock' appear. Take your finger and slide in the direction of the arrow." She passed it over to Tomas.

"Which finger?" he asked.

"Doesn't matter. Just not the one covered in jelly, please, although the screen's washable. Kids use these all the time."

As Maria helped their son into his chair, Tomas slid the white bar and a picture of Manny in the bakery appeared. He held it up for his son to see. "See Manny? It's you."

Manny continued to crunch one leg of his gingerbread man, but watched the screen.

Mel leaned over. "Now, see this arrow in the middle of the picture? Touch it with your finger and the story will start."

Sure enough, it did. They all sat and listened and watched as the story of Manny at the bakery unfolded.

"Thank you very much. It's an amazing machine," said Maria. "Manny likes his story."

Mel stood up. "When you're done with the iPad, just leave it behind the counter. Ellie will get it to me or Ben when we're back tomorrow or the next day."

"Don't you need it tonight?"

"Nah, we're good. Keep it with you just in case you need it." She circled the table to where Manny was digging off the gingerbread man's icing eyes. "High five, buddy." She held up her hand.

Maria and Tomas watched, fearful that their son was going to be rude to this helpful woman. But Mel just crouched there patiently, her eyes not leaving Manny's face.

Tomas made to reach for Manny's arm to guide his hand to meet Mel's. Mel turned her face just a fraction towards Tomas and shook her head no.

Another few seconds passed. Manny did not look directly at Mel, but raised his hand to lightly tap hers.

Mel grinned. "Good boy." To his parents, "See you guys."

CHAPTER ELEVEN

Soon, the gingerbread man was demolished and even the crumbs licked up by damp fingers. Full and satisfied, they got ready to depart. Maria set Mel's iPad behind the counter confident that all was well.

"Don't you need it?" asked Ellie.

"No, we played it for Manny a before he ate his cookie. He liked it. Thank Mel for loaning it to us, please."

Tomas held the door open for his family. Manny, holding his mama's hand went first. Then, he froze. The familiar street looked different. While they ate, a sprinkling of rain had come down, making the asphalt glisten in the street lights. Seen through Manny's eyes, yes things did look different.

But, they'd walked this route many a time, and he'd listened to the story on the iPad. It wasn't like they were asking the little guy to navigate the route home on his own.

Tomas used the hand not holding the door to push between his son's shoulder blades.

Manny's little sneakers were Crazy-Glued to the ground.

"Come on, son. It's time to go." Tomas pushed harder while Maria gave a gentle tug to his hand.

Nope, Manny was having none of it.

Sighing, Tomas realized that this approach wasn't going to work and he so did not want everyone in the bakery to witness a tantrum. He crouched on the ground behind Manny, balancing on his toes. Maybe they could get out of this gracefully. Gently he put his arms around his little boy and whispered softly, his breath tickling his son's ear.

He barely got out his soft, encouraging words when he sensed the rising tension. He heard Marie's indrawn breath as Manny's hand turned in hers, raking his nails across the thin skin on the back of her hand.

Manny rose on the balls of his feet. He raised his elbows and pushed them forward. Then with a whoosh, he pulled both his arms and head back with a force that knocked Tomas off his feet. His arms reflexively let go of his son to cradle his nose where Manny had head-butted him.

Tomas toppled and rolled on the ground holding his face; Manny perched on his toes, keening in time to his hand flapping; Mario tried ineffectually to get through to her son, while keeping a safe distance from his arms. Mostly, she blocked the street. Once, Manny had panicked and ran off in a grocery store, causing his parents minutes of heart-stopping terror before they found him.

Ellie and Jeff appeared by Tomas's side. Ellie offered Tomas a handful of napkins as Jeff helped him to his feet.

"Wow, your kid sure packs a whollup," said Jeff with admiration. "I wasn't half that strong at his age."

Tomas just looked at him. He used the napkins to wipe away the blood trickling onto his lip from his nose. There wasn't really a lot of blood, but his nose sure hurt like blazes.

Ellie pushed past the men to crouch near Manny.

"Wait," said Tomas. "Don't get so close to him." He so didn't want anyone else to get hurt by Manny.

Without looking at him, Ellie waved Tomas off. "It's fine. I'm fast," she assured him.

"Manny, look," she said. "I've got your story." Ellie had pressed the start button as she walked over and the story was already almost done. But that was enough to snag Manny's attention. He stayed on his toes and his hands still flapped, but his noises reduced in speed and decibels.

Now that she'd snagged Manny's attention, Ellie held the iPad out to Maria. "Here," she said. "Play it again for him."

Maria wedged herself between Ellie and Manny, just in case. Holding the iPad close to her son, she pressed play.

Manny's heels came down and he stilled as he watched the short video play out. When it was over, he removed two fingers from his mouth and pressed the play button.

"Here, you hold it now," Ellie told Tomas. "Mel used to make sure Kyle knew that instructions came from both she and Ben."

Tomas did as instructed, grateful to Mel for thinking to revise the story to add an ending about walking home by the light of the streetlights with his parents. When the story came to an end, Manny seemed less tense, but his feet were still rooted half in, half out of the bakery.

"Play it again," suggested Ellie.

They did and one more time and yet another. Manny relaxed visibly.

When it was over, he faced in the correct direction of home, gripped his mama's hand and, without looking, held out his other for his papa. Tomas gratefully passed the iPad to Ellie with a heartfelt, "Thanks."

It was peaceful walking through the darkened streets and Manny seemed content. It took his parents far longer to release the tension in their bodies.

"Well, that went well," quipped Maria.

"All but one little blip at the end. Still, it could have been much worse."

"Far worse." She reached her free hand over to brush the side of her husband's face. "How's your nose?"

"It's fine. Although now I have more appreciation for what you went through the time Manny broke your nose. I know how mine feels and it's definitely not broken."

"But really, what happened there was small potatoes compared to what might have happened. Do you think if we'd played that story again for him before we hit the door, he might have been more prepared?'

"Who knows? Well, Mel must have suspected that there might be problems."

They walked another half block before Tomas said, "Kind of makes you wonder why we haven't done things like this before, you know, gotten out and met people. We basically holed up in our apartment for a good part of Manny's life."

They both thought about the reasons why they'd stuck to themselves, afraid of going out in public in case their son created a scene, the kind that had become all too frequent.

A scene. Other than today, when had the last one been? They used to come almost daily, but this week? Well, the last one was the day Tomas lost his job due to Maria's call for help. Sure, there had been smaller blips along the way, but nothing that erupted into major violence. And the incident today was actually minor in comparison to the upsets they'd lived through.

Maria remarked on this. "Manny's been good lately, better, don't you think? Was your afternoon with him all right?"

"Fine. Or, mostly fine. He got frustrated when his tower toppled too many times, but nothing we couldn't manage. You're right. Things have been better lately. I wonder what's made the change."

"We haven't been cooped up in the house so much. Do you think that could make a difference to him?"

"Maybe it makes a difference to us, especially to you. You were stuck inside far too often. I know you had no choice when I was at work and it's been rough on you."

"We were fine, Tomas, although I admit that this is much nicer, these walks and going to the bakery and talking to people. Do you think Manny likes it, too? Is that why he's calmer because he's getting out and doing different things?"

"I never thought of it before. Do you think it's possible that a kid like Manny could get bored?"

With a sleepy Manny bathed, cuddled and tucked into bed, Maria and Tomas had time to themselves. In bed, with the lights out, Maria broached the subject that had been on her mind.

"Tomas, what do you know about autism?"

"Not much. I saw that old movie, Rainman when I was a kid. I think on television I've seen scenes of people who rock back and forth, bang their heads, and are lost in their own worlds. Why?"

"Because several people now have mentioned autism and Manny. I think they think that he's autistic."

"No, that can't be. No. They don't know our son. He's not hopeless like those people."

"You know Jeff - the guy at the bakery who cooks and fixes computers?"

"Yeah, didn't they introduce him as Mel's brother?"

"Yes. He has autism."

"No, that's not right. He can't."

"He told me so himself today. He seems definite about it. And, he says that Kyle, Mel's son has autism also." Maria shifted her head on Tomas's shoulder so she could look at his face in the moon light. "He says that all people with autism are different and that that view I had of autism is only one part, a small part of autism. Jeff says that autism is just one of his characteristics."

"I've seen Kyle there. He seems like every other kid."

"According to Jeff, he's a kid who has autism."

They were silent for a while. Then, Tomas asked, "What makes him think that Manny could have autism?"

"Jeff asked me why I thought Manny rocked and flapped his hands, didn't talk and made noises."

Tomas digested this information. "Why do you think he does those things?"

"I don't know. I never thought about the why of it. I just thought that that was Manny and he was different than other kids. I hoped that he'd grow out of it."

"But, he isn't, is he?"

Maria sighed. "No, I so want to believe that he is, that he's getting better and will soon be just like the children I see out the window. But, he's not. He's just not. And, I can't seem to make him better."

Tomas pulled her into his arms. "Querida, you are the best mother any child could ever have. This, this problem with Manny, it's bigger than both of us. We're doing the best we can."

"I asked Jeff that if Manny did have autism, would he ever be like Jeff. He said that Manny will need help - special help. It sounded like more than we can do for him, but stuff that people like Mel know.

"Then, he asked me why Manny is not in school."

CHAPTER TWELVE

Maria hovered. She was never a dithering sort of woman and the way she hovered just out of arms reach of their son got on Tomas' nerves. She trailed after Manny, looking more like a timid mouse than his Maria. Her hushing sounds and hesitant vibes were making both the males in her life edgy. They'd had a few rough days with Manny. Maybe they'd grown complacent and let their guards down. Now, they were back to walking on tenterhooks.

The first of the month was almost here. Tomas, usually a most patient man, was short-tempered at home. When several of Manny's blocks escaped from their teetering tower, toppling onto the newspaper, Tomas snapped at his son to, "Get those blocks out of here and leave me alone!" With a shake of the paper, he returned to his study of the want ads.

Unused to that tone from his parents, Manny stiffened. Maria feared that he was going to shriek back or even attack. Maria approached gingerly, but placed her hands on her little boy's shoulders and squeezed softly. Manny raised the blocks and let them fly with a yell. Maria ducked, but then pressed down firmly on his shoulders, as she had seen Mel do. The reaction was not immediate, but some of the tension left the child's body and his arms lowered. After staying that way for a minute, she helped Manny gather up his blocks and move them to his favorite spot in front of the window. The sun beams wouldn't appear until later in the afternoon, but for now, this might let Tomas read the paper in peace.

For the past several days, Tomas and Paul had showed up at a day worker place. How it worked was that men looking for a job registered at the office, then as jobs opened up for an hour or two or for the day, those at the front of the line would pile into the waiting truck and get a ride to wherever they were needed. The jobs were always menial and physically demanding but Tomas did not mind that. What he did mind was that it was temporary. When you showed up, you never knew where you might work, what you might be doing, the hours, or worse, even if you'd get work that day. The latter was unacceptable to a family man with responsibilities.

Today had been one of those bad days - one where there was little call for day workers and most of the men in line had been sent home. Tomas was just a few behind the lucky ones who had gotten work. Now, he was home, searching for some sort of job, anything to apply for. His concentration was broken by the telephone.

Maria hurriedly got it, giving a soft, "Hello" into the receiver. She smiled when she heard who was on the other end of the line, but her smile turned into a hesitant frown. "I don't know," she said, "I'd like to help you, but there's Manny. I'll have to see what Tomas says. May I call you back?" She took down the number.

Their apartment was too small for Tomas to not have heard Maria's side of the conversation. He waited for his wife to explain.

"That was Ellie." Maria was hesitant. "She called for help. She says it's crazy at the bakery and the lunch crowd has not even started yet. She asked if I could come in to help, even if it's just for a few hours. I told her I'd have to ask you."

Tomas' face had darkened as he listened to his wife. He wanted to thump his chest and do the 'I am the man of this house and I will support my family' routine. But, looking at Maria's nervous, hopeful face, he swallowed his words. She knew how he felt about the man providing for his family and the woman's place in the home. But, lately, he had not been doing such a good job of that, had he?

Ellie was a woman and she worked, but she was unmarried, with no man to look after her. Mel worked and she had Ben to support her, but Ben didn't seem to mind that his wife worked. Ellie had told them that her parents used to own the bakery, with their dad baking and their mom running the front of the shop. Growing up, all the kids had worked in the bakery, under their mother's direction.

Ellie had been good to Tomas' family, welcoming them when venturing out into public with Manny was still new to them. And, not just Ellie but the rest of her family and staff had greatly helped Tomas, Maria and Manny.

While Tomas let his thoughts wander, Maria awaited his answer. She watched the thoughts flitter across his face and knew the cultural dilemma he was facing. It was the man who went out to work, not the woman. Yet, there was an obligation to help out a friend. Maria prayed that the latter would rise to the surface as her husband weighed the issues. This was not a permanent thing, just a once-in-a-while job until Sal returned to work. Besides, it was fun. And, much as she adored being a wife and mother to her family, it felt good for the first time ever, to financially contribute to their home.

Tomas studied the paper a moment more, then his wife's expressive, black eyes. "When?" he asked.

Maria's brilliant smile was his reward. "Soon. Now. Right away," she said. "And, Ellie suggested that we all come down for lunch."

"She seems to be feeding us quite a bit."

"I don't mind. It's a break from cooking."

Surprised, Tomas asked, "I thought you loved cooking?"

"Generally, but not all the time. Sometimes it's nice to sit down to something that I didn't make myself. Jeff's a good cook and it's always different."

All this was news to Tomas. "Shall we go, then?"

"Wait. I want to try making a story for Manny." Maria drew a large stick figure, a small one in between then a shorter adult on the other side. Two lines served as a sidewalk. Then she drew these same stick figures sitting at a round table. Well, kind of sitting, if you stretched your imagination. She was not much of an artist and this was pretty hasty sketching.

But, Manny was an uncritical audience. When she showed him the pictures and explained that they were going to the bakery for lunch, he did not look at her nor respond. Instead, he stood, opened the closet door and tried to pull his jacket down off the hanger.

His parents watched in amazement. This was the first time he had ever gone for his coat. He understood! He had honestly understood what his mama was trying to convey. And, he responded appropriately and cooperatively.

Money might be tight, Tomas might be worried about his job prospects, but the hearts of the mother and father soared as they held their son's hands on the way to the bakery.

Maria barely had time to finish her prosciutto, Swiss cheese and cornetto sandwich before the lunch crowd enveloped the place.

"Saturdays are usually busy, but not like this," explained Ellie as she topped up Tomas' coffee. "Look," she said, "the crowd doesn't seem to bother Manny."

And, it didn't. Manny was too preoccupied trying to scoop up every crumbled piece of his rich, cornetto bread. He'd never had such a delicacy before. Neither had Tomas nor Maria. The cornetto resembled a croissant, but was not quite the same. Ellie explained that this was another of Jeff's experiments. He'd tried it out on a few people Thursday, then when it passed muster, they'd set out a sign that the Saturday special would be served on cornetto rolls.

Maria was nervous about leaving Tomas and Manny alone at the table, unsure how her son would act. It had been fine last time, but with Manny, you just never knew. And, he had never been here when there were so many people milling around.

A rattling sound approached, and then a large plastic bin plunked onto the table. It was a bucket of building blocks, carefully carried over by Kyle. Reflexively, Tomas angled his body so he could interfere in case Manny lashed out at this little boy.

"Hi," said Kyle. "Wanna play?"

It wasn't totally clear who he was speaking to. He made direct eye contact with none of the table's inhabitants, but seemed to address the air above their table. Ellie, more used to her nephew, asked him, "Who are you talking to?"

Kyle raised his eyes to his aunt. His expression said what he thought of that question. "Him," he said, pointing at Manny.

"Do you know that him has a name?" asked Ellie.

"Aunt Ellie, you are silly sometimes. Of course, he has a name. Everyone has a name."

"But do you know what his name is?"

Kyle shook his head.

"Kyle, I'd like you to meet Manny. Manny, this Kyle." Then, to Kyle, she asked, "Can you give Manny a high five?"

Kyle raised his hand and waited and waited and waited without flinching. Manny finally moved his hand into position and made contact. Although the adults heard the slap, they were impressed with the accuracy of a child who could find the hand without looking directly at it or its owner.

As Kyle stood on his toes to open the bucket, Tomas and Maria held their coffee cups in the air to make more room on the miniscule table.

"Whoa, there. Do you think there's enough room on this table top for any of the creations you build?" asked Ellie.

That gave Kyle pause.

Ellie nodded to the carpet in the corner, the one with roads and city blocks printed on it. "Why don't you guys go over there to play?"

"Okay." And, Kyle was off.

Tomas protested. "I don't really think..."

At the same time, Maria, "This is not a good idea." Tomas let his wife finish. "Manny does not play with other children."

"Doesn't he like blocks?" Ellie questioned.

"It's not that," said Tomas. "He's never played with other kids."

Tomas looked up as Mel joined their group. "Maybe this is a good time for him to start, then," she said.

Maria said quietly, "You don't understand. Sometimes Manny can be rough. We would not want him to hurt your son."

"I don't want my son to be hurt either, but I think Kyle can hold his own," said Mel. "Look. Would it help if I stayed with the boys while they played?"

"We do not want to impose," started Tomas. He was thinking that he didn't want this nice lady to get hurt either.

"Oh, it's nothing. I'll enjoy it as much as the boys." Mel stood and held out her hand to Manny. "Want to come play?"

While Tomas was still forming his protest, Manny climbed off his chair, and taking Mel's hand, followed her to the floor mat in the corner where Kyle had already dumped out the bucket of building blocks.

Manny looked at the blocks that were so familiar to him. Never before had he seen these colorful blocks outside of his own home. And, at that home, he was pretty much the only person who ever touched them. His parents knew better than to interfere with Manny's blocks and tower building. Now, here was this other child taking control of the blocks.

"Here," said Kyle as he swept an arm through the middle of the pile, shoving half towards Manny. "These are for you and these are mine."

Manny's one fist entered his mouth, while the other hand rose and flapped. His body began to rock back and forth and a low sound came from his mouth. Observing this, Tomas brought his coffee cup over to Mel's table by the carpet. "May I?" he asked, gesturing at one of the vacant chairs.

"Sure. Worried, are you?"

"Manny has those blocks at home and doesn't like anyone touching them."

"This is a good experience for him then."

Tomas sighed. "You don't understand. My son can be unpredictable. He gets upset."

"He's a kid."

With his eyes not leaving his son's swaying body, Tomas confessed. "Sometimes he lashes out. You can't always tell when it's going to happen." There. He'd said it.

Mel reached over and gave his forearm a quick squeeze. "It's okay. I understand. And, I'll watch the boys closely." Her eyes said that she did get it, but Tomas was doubtful. How could she? He had to try to make her see what could happen, what might well happen.

Painfully, eyes on the carpet, shoulders slumped, he started. "He hurts, well, sometimes he has hurt his mother." He could not meet her gaze. "It's not Maria's fault - she is a wonderful, loving mother. I do not know why he does it. And, sometimes it goes on for a long time and she can't make him stop. When it's really bad, she had to call me at work and I'd come home to rescue her. That's why I lost my job; I had to leave too many times."

"That's tough."

"But what could I do? He's getting bigger and a couple times he really hurt his mama. Once we had to go to the hospital to get the bleeding stopped."

"You're right. Safety comes first."

Now that he'd started, the dam burst and he couldn't contain the words burbling out of his mouth. "It's been better these last few weeks, or at least mostly. Maybe it's because I'm home more now. And, we've been getting out more, coming here and going for more walks."

Mel nodded. "A change of scenery can help all of you. And, Manny's been good at the bakery."

"We never thought we could do something like this with him. It got so we avoided going out in public with him in case he'd make a scene. But, that also meant that Maria was trapped in the house most of the time."

"Do you know what it is that upsets him?"

"No! If I knew what it was, I'd make it go away!"

"Make it go away? Well, it would be nice if we could smooth the path for our children that way, but it's not very practical, is it?" When Tomas didn't respond, she continued. "Sometimes, the best we can do is teaching our kids how to handle frustrations because we can't follow them around in life, fixing their problems for them."

This woman didn't get it. "But that won't work with Manny. I can't talk to him."

"You can't? Kyle doesn't seem to be having a problem talking to your son."

Their attention turned to the boys.

Their play had started out with Kyle building a car out of his share of the blocks and running it down a street on the carpet. Manny, after watching Kyle and then inspecting every square inch of one particular block returned to his usual stacking. His tower now teetered precariously. Tomas tensed, ready to spring into action if Manny let loose when his stack invariably toppled over.

Just then, Kyle's car, accompanied by the engine noises Kyle was making, plowed into the base of Manny's tower. "Kerpow!" bellowed Kyle triumphantly.

There was a moment of silence. Manny stiffened. Tomas braced for action. Across the room, Maria tensed, cradling a bin of dishes to her side. Her grip bent the plastic. Mel readied herself to intervene if necessary.

The silence was broken by Kyle's delighted giggle. He threw himself to the floor on his back, rolling both ways on the floor, laughing. His next roll pushed him against Manny's legs. Kyle's swaying arms reached out, wrapped around Manny's waist and pulled him to the ground to roll with him. Kyle was having a jolly old time.

Tomas stepped forward to disentangle the boys in case Manny lashed out. Mel watched intently. She put out a restraining hand. "Wait," she whispered to Tomas.

In a few more seconds, they both heard it, low and soft under Kyle's rambunctious laughter, but it was there all the same. A rarely-used laugh came from Manny's half squished body. He no longer resisted the rolling from Kyle, but participated in swaying them back and forth. As the boys turned toward the adults, they glimpsed Manny's face. His mouth was wide open, his head thrown back and his clear brown eyes sparkled. He was happy!

Tomas waved to Maria to come over. He had seen his son serene in sleep. He'd seen him angry. He'd seen him cuddle sleepily with his mom. He'd seen him content or engrossed in his own play. But never, ever had he seen him take such enjoyment in being with another person. After all he and Maria had tried to do for their son, it took one small boy that they hardly knew to bring out this side of their kid.

Maria rested one hand on Tomas' shoulder and stood behind his chair, astounded at the spectacle in front of her. There was her son, rolling on the floor, playing with another child. At that moment, he looked just like any other kid.

Suddenly, Kyle let go of Manny and sat up. "Let's do it again," he said, and proceeded to stack Manny's blocks.

Maria sucked in a breath. Kyle was touching the blocks that Manny had been using. She knew what usually happened when she touched Manny's blocks.

Manny righted himself to a sitting position. With a scowl and fingers in his mouth, he watched Kyle. The "ah, ah, ah" sound came from his throat and he bounced himself up and down on his knees. Before he could work himself up too badly, Kyle said, "Here." He handed Manny the wheeled vehicle he'd built out of the blocks. "Your turn." When Manny didn't take the car, Kyle thrust it farther into Manny's space. "Take it," he instructed.

Manny reached out for the car. He turned it over and over, and then raised it over his head with one hand. The fingers of his other hand came out of his mouth and his index finger delicately spun the front wheels. And spun them and spun them.

Kyle, meanwhile, grew impatient. "Come on, you knock it down now." When Manny didn't comply, Kyle grasped Manny's outstretched arm, and lowered it to the carpet. He made a pretend motion with his other hand, urging Manny to take down the tower.

Again, Tomas rose to assist his son. Ben, Kyle's dad had come over to see what Mel was watching so intently. In a low voice, he said to Tomas, "Hang on a sec. Let's see how this plays out. We can separate them fast enough if things get out of control, but the boys might figure it out on their own."

And, he was right. Kyle ran an imaginary car back and forth across the carpet, racing up to the tower, but stopping just short of a collision, all the while making zoom, zoom noises.

Manny placed the car on the carpet and imitated Kyle's motions. Kyle grinned at him and instructed, "Okay, now!"

Manny let loose the car with enough force to explode the blocks across the carpet. Once again Kyle's giggling and rolling started, capturing Manny in a bear hug of joy. This time, Manny hugged back, and then the game began again.

"Amazing," said Tomas when he felt he could breathe again.

The lull in the bakery crowd allowed Maria to observe up close for a few moments. She and Tomas entwined hands under the table. "I dreamed, but never thought I'd see the day when Manny played, actually played with another child."

"We celebrate our successes where we find them." Mel and Ben shared a smile. Then she raised an eyebrow at her husband, with a nod toward the boys. "Sure," Ben mouth back as he lowered himself to the carpet with the kids.

Mel motioned Tomas and Maria to a nearby table. "You can still see Manny from here, and Ben will watch them." To Maria, she said, "Looks like the crowd has slowed down for a bit."

As they settled in the chairs, Mel faced Tomas. "You mentioned that while things have generally been better lately, there are still some rough patches." He nodded. "Do you mind if I ask you about them?"

Tomas's back straightened. "We handle it and we look after our son."

Maria intervened. "I think that Mel is saying that she might have some ideas for us to try. Right?"

"Look, if you don't mind my interference, I might have some suggestions that could help you and help Manny. I've been through this myself as a parent and I've had lots of experience with kids."

"You have been most kind to us. Certainly, we would like to hear what you have to say." Tomas became stiffly formal when he started into his defensive mode.

Mel studied him carefully. "Well", she began, "life can be especially frustrating for kids who don't talk. They have no way to make their wants and needs known. Often, it's up to the parents to play a guessing game;

sometimes we're not very good at it, frustrating the kid even more. That's when he might lash out. Does Manny ever seem to want something and you don't know what it is?"

"Oh, yeah," said Maria. "Sometimes I'd give him anything, anything at all, if I could just figure out what it is he's after." She turned to Tomas. "Remember yesterday? He must have been hungry and fancied something, but every snack I offered just seemed to make him madder."

Tomas nodded. "We see this often, but don't know what to do. If only he'd just say what it is he's after."

"Sometimes we use pictures with kids who can't speak to us. Look, here's what I mean." Mel pulled up some pictures on her iPad. "This is just a very simple choice board, but pictured here is a glass of milk and a glass of orange juice. The child can point to the drink he prefers." She quickly scrolled through more pictures. "Here's one that shows three kinds of cereal." She scrolled some more. "This one's not about food, but gives the child a choice of either wearing a blue shirt or a green one." That may not seem like a big deal, but so much of life is out of the control of these children; having even a small say, such a choice in what he wears can be empowering."

Maria moved her finger through a few more choice boards. "Some of these have like ten different pictures to choose from."

"Yes, and some have many more than that. But when we're first getting a child used to the idea, we usually just stick with two or at the most, three pictures."

"This is very nice, but we do not have a computer or an iPad," said Tomas.

"You don't need either. What you do need are pictures. In fact, I wouldn't recommend starting with pictures on an iPad. Who wants to have to carry this thing around all day? Instead, you might want to put a couple pictures on the fridge. Or, start a book of pictures, sort of like a choice book."

Maria and Tomas sat mulling over the possibilities.

Encouraging them, Mel asked, "What does Manny like to eat? You mentioned snacks. What are his favorite snacks?"

"Grapes," said Maria.

"Green ones," added Tomas, "definitely not the purple kind. We made that mistake once. We learned that our son is for sure not color-blind."

"I think Ellie has some grapes in the display case," said Mel and she left with her iPad. At the counter, she asked to borrow a cluster of grapes and, placing them on a white, paper napkin, took a photo of the fruit.

"What else?" she asked.

"Crackers," said Maria, "but only this kind." She pulled a small package from her purse. "I always carry some, just in case."

Mel smoothed out another napkin and took a shot of the crackers. "Now, I'll just print these for you." She fiddled with her iPad, mumbling something about air printing, and then went to find her brother, Jeff.

In minutes, the printer in the corner spit out two color pictures of Manny's favorite snacks. Mel thanked Jeff who complained that she really needed to take the time to learn how to do some of these things on her own.

Mel, like a practiced sibling, ignored him. "Now, you can tape these to your fridge or put them someplace handy when you want Manny to choose a snack." Then, she added a caution. "But, you can't expect him to just know what this is all about. You have to teach him."

"Thank you, but we are not teachers."

"Parents are their kids' first and their best teachers. What I mean is, you are going to have to practice with Manny, show him over and over what these pictures mean and how to make choices. You might need to place actual grapes on top of the picture so he makes the connection. Maybe give him a cracker as you show him the corresponding picture. Do this over and over. You might need to hold up both a cracker and a grape and ask him which he wants. He might catch on to the picture representations, but you might need to begin with the actual objects, and then move on to the pictures. Over time, he'll come to see that he has some power and the ability to make choices.

"Later, we can add in more and more pictures and of more things than just food."

"I appreciate your time, but we do not want our son spending his life pointing at pictures. We do not want him to rely on such things. What we really prefer is that he just talk."

"Definitely! That is the goal. Please believe me that using pictures will not prevent or delay your son from speaking. Talking is so much less work, that if and when he does begin using words, they are so much faster and easier, that he'll leave these pictures behind.

"In the meantime, having a communication system can decrease some of the frustration and powerlessness he might feel – you know, those kinds of feelings that can lead to aggression." Mel regarded Maria and Tomas steadily. "Manny will only get bigger. And stronger. The more you can do to reduce his frustration and his aggression, the better off he'll be and the better off you'll all be. Believe me, been there, done that."

"Kyle seems like such an easy child," Maria said with a note of wistfulness.

"Huh," said Mel. "You might not have said that a couple years ago."

The three adults shifted their attention to the ruckus in the corner, their spider senses now alert to the slight change in timbre. Ben moved from the sidelines to the middle of the excited fray.

Mel's look was rueful. "I don't want to burst your bubble, but I think our good times are almost over."

Ben said over his shoulder to them, "I recognize that tone in Kyle's laughter. He's about to turn from sweet to over-stimulated."

Tomas and Maria looked confused.

"Kyle's good for a certain amount of time but when he's tired that time is shorter and he had a restless night last night. I think we'd better pull the pin on this." He looked at Mel. "Do you want to do the honors, or shall I?"

"But the boys are having fun," protested Maria.

Mel nodded at Ben to interrupt the boys' game while she explained to Manny's parents. "When Kyle gets too wound up, he can't easily calm himself. We can tell by the sound of his laughter - it becomes shrill. Then, instead of winding down, he gets going faster and harder until the laughing turns into screaming and things aren't fun at all for him. Or us. It takes much longer to get him into a calmer state if we let this go on for too long."

"How do you stop it?"

Mel laughed. "Sometimes, not easily. It depends. If we catch things soon enough, we can often distract him and get him going on something else that quiets him. Today, I'm not sure. It might be harder since he's not at home. Also, he was genuinely enjoying himself with your son and may not want to stop. Brace yourself; this might not be pretty."

"If he protests, will you let him continue playing some more?" She was hoping Manny could continue to play this wondrous game with this miracle boy.

Mel looked quizzically at Maria. "No, if we tell him it's time to stop, then it's time to stop."

Tomas said, "If that was Manny and we tried to make him stop something he wanted to do, we might have a tantrum on our hands."

"Yes," agreed Mel. "That's a possibility. Then what would you do?"

"We'd likely leave him for a bit then try again later," said Maria. "That's usually what we do when we want to get him into bed at night."

Mel leaned forward, resting her bent elbow on the table and her chin on her fist. "How does that work for you?"

Tomas laughed. "Well eventually he gets to bed every night."

"I hope you don't mind my asking. It's the teacher in me, please understand. So, what do you think Manny learns from that?"

"I guess that if he waits us out, he can play a bit longer, but eventually he'll have to go to bed." Tomas thought a moment more. "Sometimes he falls asleep on top of his blocks, and then we undress him and put him to bed."

Ben walked up with a giggling, but more subdued Kyle firmly clamped and slung upside down over one shoulder. "Huh," he said. "Been there, done that. I used to do anything, anything at all, not to have this kid scream. At least, that was before Mel came into our lives. Now the screaming is rarer and Kyle knows the rules and the routines."

"Most of the time," added Mel. "We're all still part of a work in progress."

Ben twisted Kyle around so that he rested against Ben's chest. "I think we'd better get this young man home. I see a bath, hot chocolate and a bed time story in his immediate future."

"Hot chocolate," mumbled Kyle from the vicinity of his dad's neck.

Mel pushed back her chair and grabbed the bucket of blocks the boys had cleaned up with Ben. She squatted down to eye level with Manny. Quietly, she said, "Kyle had fun playing with you. Maybe you can come to our house one day to play with him again. Will you give me a high five?"

While she spoke, Manny's rocking stopped. His eyes did not move from a spot on the carpet, but he held his hand aloft. Mel gently slapped his palm, and then gave his hand a squeeze. "See you," she said.

"Are you going to work some more?"

"No," answered Maria. "I think Ellie's okay now that things have died down. It was pretty hectic there for a while."

Worriedly, Tomas asked, "Was it too much for you? You don't have to do this, even if she is a friend."

Maria hurried to reassure him. "Tomas, I love it. It's fun to be part of the team making things happen here. It is work I can do and it's interesting and I like meeting the people who come in here."

"Well, if you're sure you're not getting over-tired. But, this was a one-time thing anyway."

Maria frowned. "Yes, she just asked me to come in today, that's right. But Sally will be off for a few more weeks. I know you don't want me working, but it's just a few hours a day for the next couple weeks and it would really help Ellie out. I don't know how she would have coped if I had not come in. There would not have even been clean dishes for the customers to eat from."

Watching the carpet, Tomas changed gears. Manny gently swayed back and forth in his sitting position, sucking on his fingers, with his eyes at half-mast. "Let's talk about this more tomorrow. For now, I think we have our own young man to get home."

Although Manny sometimes did not want physical contact, tonight he didn't object when his papa hoisted him up, cradling his gangly frame. Manny's head rested on Tomas's shoulder, his arms limp at his side, his legs dangling. Tomas shifted the weight to get a better grip and settle his son more comfortably.

Quietly, Maria and Tomas waved good-bye to Ellie and Jeff and went out into the night.

Both parents were pensive for the first part of the walk home. Then, Maria asked, "What did you think about what Ben and Mel were saying about Kyle getting over-excited?"

"Yeah, Manny does that, too. But with him it's not from playing with anyone, but from some game he has going with himself."

"Do you think you can tell when he's going to get out of control?"

"Maybe sometimes, but not always."

"Do you think we could stop it when we notice the signs?"

"We've never really tried, have we?"

Maria admitted, "I'm always afraid of making it worse or having him lash out at me."

"We're in a bad position. If we don't do anything and let things build up, then he gets really going and his world just erupts. If we tried to interrupt things and head it off, would we be any better off than if we let him be?"

"I guess we could try, but I'd rather do it when the two of us are there with him," said Maria.

Tomas squeezed her hand. "I want both my wife and my son safe." They walked on another half block. "That was interesting what Ben said about how he used to do anything to keep Kyle from screaming."

"I can hardly picture that in the Kyle we see at the bakery."

"You know, I think I get the point Mel was making. What Manny is learning is that when we tell him to do something and he kicks up a fuss, then he gets his way."

"You're right. If he yells or throws things, we don't make him take his bath or come for lunch if he doesn't want to. We wait until he's ready."

"If he's ever ready."

Maria laughed. "You're right."

"Maybe we can talk to Mel about this another time. She's a teacher and teachers are used to handling bunches of kids, where we just have experience with this one."

"Did you hear what she said to Manny when she knelt on the carpet with him?"

"No, I didn't catch that. I was talking to Ben."

"You won't believe this. She told him that Kyle had fun playing with him and said that maybe Manny could come to their house to play with him."

CHAPTER THIRTEEN

"Here goes," said Maria. She held up a picture green grapes in her left hand and red grapes in her right.

"Manny," called Tomas. "Come see what your mama has for you." When Manny didn't glance up from his blocks, Tomas went and took him by the hand, gently pulling him to his feet then to the kitchen.

At first Manny stood beside his papa, fingers in his mouth, eyes roving about the room. Instructions to look at the pictures had little effect as Manny's glance slid by them.

Maria knelt down, placing the picture directly in front of her son. "Manny, would you like some grapes? Which ones do you want?"

Manny tilted his head back to get a better look. Maria moved them not quite so close to his face. First Manny studies the photo of the green grapes. His finger left his mouth and started to approach that picture. Then his gaze moved to the other picture. He shrieked and his wet fingers stabbed at the offending red grape representation. And, the melt-down began.

"So much for that idea." Tomas sighed and collapsed on the couch. "We will not do that again. Why not just give him the green grapes? We'd have saved ourselves half an hour of grief."

"I wonder if we should have used pictures of just things he likes, maybe green grapes and crackers?"

"Are you up for trying it again?"

"Nope, not me!" At least not now, Maria thought. It could be avoided no longer. The first of the month announced itself and the rent was due. Tomas was almost silent during breakfast, girding himself to go talk to their landlord. Pleading for extra time to come up with the full rent money so went against his principles and his pride. Never had they been late before. And, so far his prospects of getting full-time work were bleak.

He looked around their apartment. It was small, yes. Was it ideal? Far from it. A child needed room to play outside in the fresh air and sunshine, but that just was not possible in their third floor walk-up. Sure, Maria kept the place spotless and decorated it as prettily as she could on their budget. And, the neighborhood was good. Tomas need not worry about the safety of his family when he was gone.

If he had trouble coming up with the rent money this month and next, would they be evicted? Then what? While this place was tiny, at least they had two bedrooms. Well, not exactly two, but Manny's bed was in the large walk-in storage closet, plenty big enough for a small bed and dresser. If they had to move, it would be to a smaller place still. Manny would have to sleep with them or in the living room. Could Tomas go to work, leaving his family alone during the day if they lived in some of the more questionable neighborhoods? Maria would truly be a prisoner in the apartment.

But, wasn't she now? She was afraid to take Manny out of the apartment by herself, and with good reason. There was that time when she took him to the store for some milk. She never knew what upset him, but suddenly he threw himself to the floor in a full-on yelling, shrieking, kicking tantrum. His hands snatched items from the nearest shelves and threw them. When his mama bent to him, Manny grabbed the jug of milk from her hands and tossed it. Landing on the edge of a shelf, the container broke, spewing milk all over the floor, the stocked shelves and Manny. The feel of the cold liquid on his face momentarily silenced the child, and then he let loose with sounds that dragged over customers from all over the store. Maria could not make him stop. She could not pick him up. She could not get him to stand up and walk out of the building with her. Dragging him by one arm along the floor occurred to her desperate mind, but she could not do that in front of all these people. So, she continued to plead and soothe, all to no effect. She'd intersperse this with attempts to restock the shelves but nothing helped. When Manny got like this, there was nothing to be done but let him wind himself down. Maria suffered the accusing stares of the onlookers and all their unsolicited advice.

By the time he wound down, he was exhausted, as was his mother. He did eventually allow Maria to lead him out of the store. She half walked, half carried her tired boy the three, oh so long blocks home. They never did get the milk and never again did Maria enter a store alone with Manny.

His wife was too often trapped inside this apartment. But she was not even safe there. Tomas had lost track of the number of times Maria had phoned him for help when Manny attacked her. And, there were countless more times that he'd come home to find fresh bruises or cuts on his beautiful wife when Manny had hurt her.

Maria interrupted his reverie. "Tomas, you're so quiet. What is it?"

Looking into her eyes hurt. It was his duty to protect and care for his wife and child and he had failed. First, he had failed to instill in their son the values of respecting women, in particular your mother. He had not taught his son well and he had not protected his wife from their son's rages. Then he had failed to provide for his family. He lost his job and could not find another. Now, he would have to admit that there was not enough money to cover their rent. What kind of a man would get into this position?

He took Maria's soft hand in both of his. "I am so sorry, querida. I have let you and our son down. Today our rent is due and I do not have enough money to cover it."

Maria stood up and walked toward the kitchen counter. "How much are we short?"

As Tomas named the sum, Maria withdrew the sugar bowl from the cupboard and brought it to the table. She dumped it upside down and began smoothing out the crumpled bills. "I bet we have enough in here."

Tomas had forgotten the stash that Maria had been saving. While he helped stack and count the bills, Maria took off for the hall closet. She dug in her coat pocket and came back with an envelope containing more bills, these ones carefully folded.

"What's that?"

"It's my pay!" Maria was so excited. "I told Ellie I would just help her out as a friend, but she would not let me lift a plate without agreeing that I'd be paid for the work, the way she pays everyone who helps there. She said it's not much, just minimum wage, but is it enough to help with the rent?"

Tomas's face darkened. He was to provide for his family. That was the man's job, not the woman's.

Maria's words rushed in. "Ellie said to consider it fun money, just a little something for extras and to compensate for my time." She looked to see her husband's reaction. "I know I can't make the kind of money you do and could never support anyone, but maybe I can help out just a little?" Her voice rose at the end of the sentence.

Tomas's emotions warred within him. A wife working for pay went against every chivalrous value he'd been raised with. It made him less of a man if he could not provide for the family he'd created. But looking at Maria's pleading, shining eyes, he bit back the angry, insulted words that were percolating too close to the surface. He needed to think before saying something too quickly. How could he wipe that hopeful expression from Maria's face?

"Tomas, I want to help, too. Will you please let me?"

Things were different here. Ellie working didn't count since she wasn't married and had no man to look after her. But, Mel worked and Ben didn't seem to mind. Many women held down jobs in this country. But, it was not his way and not the way he'd been raised. Still....

Maria shoved the sugar bowl stack of money closer to Tomas. "This is your money, bits that I saved from the housekeeping money you gave me. Sometimes you were too generous and we did not need all of that so I stored it in here."

His beautiful, smart wife. He took the envelope she offered. "We only need to add some of this to what I already have to make the rent. Thank you, querida."

"Wait! There's more." Maria left the room and came back with her purse. "I know this isn't much, but it is payment Ellie gave me for selling the churros. I thought we'd use this for a treat for ourselves."

"A treat at the bakery?"

"We'd be fools not to."

Since it was Sunday, there wasn't much Tomas could do to further his job hunting, other than checking Saturday night's classified ads. So, it was a good time to go spend their treat money.

As they walked, Tomas asked, "Did you expect to get paid for making those churros?"

"Not initially. I thought I was baking them to show Ellie what churros were. But once she and Jeff tasted them, they wanted to offer them to their customers. Oh, Tomas, people liked them so much. Ellie said she'd pay me any time I wanted to make them."

Tomas squeezed her hand before responding. He needed to gather his thoughts. "Do you want to do it again?" he asked carefully.

"Sure, when I have time. I love to bake and we can only eat so much of the stuff. Why? Do you see a problem with it?"

"Noooo, I guess, as long as you're not overtaxing yourself."

"I'd only do it when I feel like it or when I'm not busy with something else."

The bakery was not yet within sight. Maria slowed her steps. "Tomas, what would you like me to do if Ellie asks me to help out again? It may not happen if she's not busy, but what should I say if she does?"

"What would you like to say?"

"I know how you feel about your wife working. But this is just a little bit of work and I would only do it when you're here to be with Manny. I do not want to work all the time - when would I get my housework done? But just sometimes, yes. And it feels good to help a friend."

"I'll leave the decision up to you then. I will have a job soon, so money will not be a problem. But if you want to work a little, I guess it's all right with me."

"Oh, Tomas, thank you, thank you." The words were muffled as her arms squeezed his neck. Giving her husband a hug in public was not something Maria usually indulged in, so Tomas knew he did the right thing.

The bell tinkled over the door to the bakery. When he saw who was entering, Ben waved them over, pulling in another table to make room for Tomas, Maria and Manny to join them. Ellie came from behind the counter to high five Manny and take him to the counter to choose his treat. This time Tomas and Maria followed after giving Ben and Mel the 'one minute' sign. Today, Manny was not the only one looking forward to a treat, but they were opting for something cream filled, rather than Manny's perennial gingerbread man.

When Maria reached for the plate containing Manny's cookie, Ellie moved it back out of Maria's reach, instead passing it down to Manny. "He can do it," she told Maria.

Manny oh so carefully followed his mother over to the Wicken family's table. Once he'd deposited his precious cargo, Mel gave instructions. "Come here, Manny, and give me a high five." Maria and Tomas held their breaths, thinking that their son would ignore this woman who was being nice to him. Mel waited without moving or speaking. It was almost ten seconds before Manny's feet moved around the table towards Mel. He did not look at her, but raised his hand. Mel gently tapped his palm, giving his fingers a gentle squeeze. "It's so nice to see you, Manny." She moved her chair back a bit to allow Ben a turn.

"Give me five, Manny," instructed Ben. Manny complied.

"And, me," said Kyle with more exuberance. Manny, standing between Kyle and Ben, had only to turn his body slightly to meet Kyle's hand. There was a resounding slap and an accompanying, "Hi, Manny!" from Kyle.

As he lowered his hand, Manny turned his head and glanced at Kyle out of the corner of his eye. He uttered a very low, "Hi."

Maria and Tomas gaped at their son and at each other. Manny had spoken. Again! That was twice now and both times in this bakery. It must be a charmed place.

Watching them, Mel said, "It'll happen more and more often now. You'll see."

As Tomas helped Manny into his chair, pushing it close to the table, Maria asked Mel how she knew this.

"I've seen it before. Sometimes other kids are the best speech therapists of all and have a way of drawing language out of each other."

"Thanks for inviting us to join you. When we walked in, you looked like you were having a serious conversation and we didn't want to interrupt."

"Mommy's worried," explained Kyle. "Mr. Tinsdale's sick and the school's dirty."

"Kyle. That's not quite right," corrected Ben. "Mr. Tinsdale's the janitor at Mel's school. He's off work indefinitely with some health problems and they're having trouble finding a replacement. They've had a couple day workers but that's not really the way to go."

Mel explained, "The way we run our school, all the adults in the building develop relationships with the kids. It doesn't work to have a different janitor there every day. We need someone we can get to know and someone to rely on. It has to be a special person too, because sometimes we have students work with the janitor."

Tomas and his wife exchanged glances. "What does a janitor have to do?"

"The usual that you'd expect - clean the floors and bathrooms, wipe off desks, do minor repairs, call in trades people when more is needed, cut the grass and clear snow at different times of the year. Kids stuff too much toilet paper down the toilets and they get clogged, so that needs to be taken care of. Little fingers leave prints on the windows. Their shoes track in dust and mud. The janitor should remind kids of the rules and doing their part in looking after the school, without getting mad at them. That was a problem with a guy who subbed in last week.

"Plus, as part of the school staff, a janitor must be there for the kids," said Mel. "That latter part is crucial. I'm the staff rep on the hiring committee and that last part was the stumbling block for our last two candidates we interviewed."

"Mel's second guessing herself, wondering if she was too stringent in her requirements, because now they have nobody," explained Ben. "They have kids with allergies to dust and stuff like that so they need someone to be looking after the place."

Trying not to look too eager, Tomas asked, "What qualifications does a person need?"

"There's no particular course; it's mainly on-the-job-training, spending a bit of time with a more experienced person in another building to learn the ropes. Of course, the person needs good all-round instincts when it comes to repairs. Having a steam engineering or boiler certificate would help, but it's not crucial. Our furnace system is pretty good and the district has a supervisor we can call in if there are problems."

Tomas, trying to hold in his excitement, attempted to portray calm confidence. He didn't want to impose on this new friendship, but this job sounded perfect for him. "Where I come from, there was no need for furnaces, so I have no experience with boiler systems. But the rest of what you describe, I can do and do well."

"My Tomas can fix anything. Even the caretaker of our building comes to get Tomas when he has trouble with some repairs," said Maria.

"Seriously?" Mel asked. "Are you saying you're interested in the job?"

"Si. Very interested."

"Would you need to give much notice before you could begin? We're looking for someone who can start quickly so we don't have to rely on a different sub each day."

With dignity, Tomas explained, "I have recently left my last position and am looking for another now. I am able to begin anytime."

"All right, then. Give me your contact information and I'll give it to the committee. You understand that because I know you, I can't be in on your interview, but I can give a recommendation. I've seen you with your son and you have the kind of patience we're looking for." When none of them came up with a piece of paper, she passed Tomas a clean napkin to write on.

CHAPTER FOURTEEN

By the end of the week, Tomas was ensconced in Madson School as the replacement janitor. It was not a permanent job; he was only there until Mr. Tinsdale's return, but the job would for sure last the rest of this school year. Then, depending on Tinsdale's health and the possibility of long-term disability, the position could turn into a permanent one for Tomas.

Although nervous, Tomas had survived the interview and thankfully, his former boss, Mr. Humber, must have given him a good recommendation. Tomas was honest about his reason for leaving his previous job, explaining that there were difficulties with his son and he had had to take time off to go help his family. Truthfully, he could say that the circumstances that caused him to need time off work had changed. He admitted that he could not guarantee that it would never happen again, there had been no incidents for several weeks now and he was hopeful that things were settling down. Luckily, there was some flexibility in his janitorial hours and if he had to leave during the day, he could return later to finish up his work.

Tomas liked working independently and felt that was his strength. He also liked order and cleanliness. Doing repair work was an interesting challenge, not a chore, so for him, the job was ideal.

Earlier in their marriage, Tomas had looked forward to being a father. He believed himself to be good with children and liked being around them. At first, he delighted in being a dad. Manny's lack of responsiveness was just an aspect of his independent personality, a sign of early maturity, his parents felt. They had a self-possessed sort of son, who was marvelous at entertaining himself. But, as he reached the toddler then preschool ages, his lack of speech grew more worrisome. Maria finally gave up on the ideal of toilet training because Manny took no interest in the process whatsoever and became increasingly upset at her efforts to get him into the bathroom.

The more Tomas and Maria compared Manny to other children they saw, the more their anxiety blossomed. Would he be one of those children who grew up in the confines of their parents' homes, growing into dependent adults, hidden away from the eyes of others? There had been a young man in their village that was that way, seldom seen or heard of, but everyone knew he was there in the back room of that one house. People there looked after their own. And, it was more protection than shame that kept such helpless people within the confines of immediate family. Yes, that was the reason he remained hidden, it must be. But their Manny would not grow up to be like that. And yet....

Manny snuggled against Maria on the couch, watching one of his favorite movies. He kept his mama's hand between his own, gently stroking her fingers. Maria kissed the top of his head and thought about some of what Mel had said about frustrations and communication.

This was a good day. Would it be a time to have another go at that choice board business? No, not when their morning was so peaceful with her little boy cuddled next to her, almost asleep. She rested her head on the back of the couch and joined Manny in a nap.

It was Manny's stirring that woke her, then his cry of irritation. Maria looked at her watch. It was almost time for Tomas to come home for lunch and she had nothing prepared. Now, Manny was fussy, just when she needed to get some food prepared.

When Manny was hungry, he did not seem to understand the concept of waiting until it was ready. His irritation was growing; if this turned into a meltdown, she would not be able to make lunch.

She glanced at the top part of the fridge where they had placed the pictures Mel took. Dare she try it now?

"Come on, son." She took Manny by the hand and led him to the fridge. She moved the pictures of the green grapes and the crackers down to the child's eye level. She knelt beside him. As his annoyed sounds grew in intensity, Maria moved her head out of range. Standing behind Manny, she took his hand and pointed at first the photo of the grapes, then the picture of crackers. She touched his hand to each picture as she labelled the food. "Which do you want, Manny? Green grapes or some crackers?"

No response. Maria touched his hand to the choices again as she named the food. Again. And yet again. He just didn't get it and was getting more impatient by the minute.

"Hang on a minute, little man." Quickly, Maria got out one cracker and one grape. She held them on top of each picture and again gave him the label for each food. As Manny started to reach for the cracker, she moved it slightly out of his reach and placed it above its picture. She restated his choices.

Manny's hand slapped the picture of the cracker. "Good boy!" Immediately, she gave him the cracker. Within seconds, it was devoured. Manny stood there waiting.

"Would you like more?" Maria held the grape and another cracker above their pictures. Manny's hand came out of his mouth and left a moist trail on the picture of the cracker. "Yes, Manny, you can have a cracker."

The next time, Manny chose the grape. Wow, thought Maria. My son can even mix it up. But, this was a one-off. The next time he went back to his crackers.

The click of a key in the lock signaled Tomas' arrival. He stopped on the threshold, listening to his son's giggle and Maria's laugh. Manny stuffed yet another cracker into his mouth.

"Watch, Tomas, watch!" Maria reached for another cracker, and asked Manny if he wanted a grape or a cracker. Manny's hand slapped the picture of a grape this time. "He gets it!" Maria's grin was huge. "It's a slow way to feed him, but he actually gets it." Then, looking at the clock on the wall, "We were having so much fun. Sorry, but I forgot about making lunch." She moved the cards from the fridge to the table and handed Tomas the next cracker and grape. "Here, you try this with him while I make some sandwiches."

A boy came wheeling down the wet hallway floor exuberantly. "Hey," he called. "Who are you?" He glided up to where Tomas stood with his mop and pail, cleaning up the evidence of hundreds of little sneakers entering the school building that morning. The child applied the wheelchair brakes unevenly, causing the chair to swerve slightly, sliding half around Tomas. Tomas reached out to steady the chair, fearful that this boy would fall out.

"Nah, I'm okay. Don't worry about me. I know how to handle this beast," the kid assured Tomas. "Hi. I'm Jordan. I'm in grade 4. Who are you?" Jordan held out his hand, a hand that didn't quite lay flat. His wrist was cocked at a ninety degree angle, with his thumb out straight and his fingers pointing back toward his inner elbow.

"Hi. I'm Tomas Garza. I'm taking Mr. Tinsdale's place as the school caretaker." He was unsure if he should shake Jordan's extended hand. Did it hurt the kid to have it bent like that? Since Jordan just waited, Tomas gingerly wrapped his around the boy's smaller hand. He was surprised at the firmness of the grip Jordan gave him.

Jordan grinned. "I'm strong, aren't I?"

Despite the fact that he was in a wheelchair, this was still a kid, Tomas realized. "Yep, you are."

Before he could admonish the child about driving his chair on wet floors, Jordan was off with one hand flap over his shoulder, and a "See ya."

Although of course he knew what a wheelchair was, Tomas had never before met a person who used one. At all other past encounters, Tomas had politely averted his eyes, so as not to be seen staring at the person or the contraption. Where he grew up, wheelchairs were rare; he couldn't think of when he'd ever noticed one.

Now, this child, Jordan, had not given Tomas time to feel awkward in the presence of someone with a handicap. He'd been in his face and confident.

"I see you've met Jordan," called Dr. Hitkin as she walked down the school hallway. "He's quite a force, isn't he?"

"I don't think he should be using that thing on wet floors. He was not very careful. He could have fallen."

"Yes, he could have and he likely will sometimes," she agreed.

"But shouldn't we stop him from doing that? He should not be allowed..." Tomas stopped. This was his first day on the job and here he was telling the principal how to run her school. Way to get fired. "I am sorry. I was worried for his safety."

"And well you might. In this building, I make the rules, but I only make rules that I can enforce. I can't stop Jordan from being a child, nor would I want to. You're quite right that he might fall out of his chair; that's a very real possibility with an energetic kid like Jordan."

"He might get hurt."

"True, he might. All boys run the risk of getting hurt in their play. Have you never fallen out of a tree when you were a kid?"

"Off a roof, in my case. But I wasn't handicapped."

"I'm not sure Jordan realizes there's a difference. He sees himself as a kid."

"Don't we need to protect him?"

"We protect each and every child in this school to the extent that we can and that it's good for them. But we encourage every student to be a child and to be themselves despite any differences they may have."

Tomas looked unconvinced.

"Dr. Hitkin said, "You'll have to come watch one day. Our OT, occupational therapist that is, comes a couple times a year and gives the kids lessons on falling. We spread out the mats in the gym and the whole class practices how to fall."

Tomas' head drew back and his eyes widened. "Not children like Jordan."

"Especially kids like Jordan. She pays extra attention to the kids who use wheelchairs, walkers or braces. They need to know how to protect themselves as best they can if they fall. Then she works with them on ways they can get back into their chair or walker with or without help. Because, we know it's going to happen, don't we? Falling is inevitable in life."

"I don't think I could allow that if Jordan was my boy."

"Mel mentioned that you have a child with special needs."

Tomas stiffened. "I have a son, yes. His name is Manny."

Dr. Hitkin smiled encouragingly. "How old is he?"

"Nine."

"What school does he go to?"

"He is not in school." Dr. Hitkin waited. With quiet dignity, Tomas explained, "He is not like other children."

"Exactly how is he not like other children?" asked Dr. Hitkin.

"Manny is fine. He is at home with his mother and we look after him." Tomas squeezed out the mop in the bucket. "Now, I must get back to my work. I will do my best at this job." And, it pays the rent, he thought.

CHAPTER FIFTEEN

"Sure, he'd have fun," assured Mel as she watched Manny and Kyle demolish their gingerbread cookies, one appendage at a time.

Maria was not convinced. "I don't know."

"He and Kyle are friends now. They do well together. Manny could sit with him and his class." At Maria's look of alarm, she amended, "Or, he could sit on a chair at the side between you and me."

Next Friday a touring company was bringing a puppet show to Madson School. Mel thought it would be a nice way of introducing Manny to the school and being around other kids.

"We don't really take him out in public. We've had some unpleasant experiences." Maria hated to make the admission but she'd grown more comfortable with Mel over the past weeks.

Mel looked around the bakery pointedly. "Isn't this a public place?"

Maria laughed. "But it's different. We're used to it now and Manny's comfortable here. He knows the routine."

"He could get used to school and the routine there as well."

"Attending one puppet show wouldn't really make him used to anything."

"It's a start."

At school, Dr. Hitkin sought out Tomas. "Have you seen the posters?" she asked.

Since he was standing right beside one, Tomas indicated it. "The kids are buzzed about it. Jordan came wheeling by yesterday, to tell me how great it's going to be."

The principal laughed. "That boy has really taken a shine to you."

"He's a good kid."

"You seem surprised."

"No, it's just that I've never known anyone handicapped before."

"I don't think Jordan sees himself as handicapped. He's a kid who just happens to get around in a wheelchair."

"But his parents must worry all the time."

"As do all parents. Yes, he could get hurt the way he uses those wheels, but how many kids are daredevils?" She raised her eyebrows. "I dare say *you* did a thing or two you didn't want your parents to find out about when you were Jordan's age."

Tomas chuckled. "I can think of a time or two or three. But that's different. I was a normal kid."

"Ouch. Don't ever let Jordan hear you say that he's not a normal kid. Can you imagine what that would do to him?" Her tone softened. "Look, I know his parents and yes, they do worry. But do they have the right to prevent him from discovering all that he can be? Do any of us as parents?"

There was silence between them for a moment, then Dr. Hitkin continued. "The reason I stopped you was to invite your wife and son to the puppet show. I think your little boy would enjoy it."

"Thank you very much, but I don't think so. Manny's never been in a school before."

"Then it's high time he was. We would love to have him and this is a great show. They come every year and we've never had a student not love it. The show's open to our students and the families of staff members. That means you."

The next day at school, Mel sought out Tomas. "Hey, I heard that you might bring Manny to the puppet show. I wondered if he'd like a story about it."

Cautiously, Tomas explained that he and Maria had not decided yet if it was a good idea for Manny to come to school. Not wanting to appear ungracious, he added, "But he does like your stories."

"Good. In case you wanted it, I've made him a story about the puppet show." She handed him a stapled booklet.

On the cover was a picture of Manny grinning with his hand raised. The title of the book was *Manny Goes to the Puppet Show*. Tomas opened the book. Each page held a large picture with a caption. The first was of Manny and Maria holding hands and smiling. The next was the outside of the school building, with the shot focusing on the entrance door. Then there was a shot of Tomas standing in the hall, waving. The facing page said, "We walk down the hall to the gym" with an angled shot of the hallway plus the gym door. From previous assemblies, Mel had added a picture of students sitting in the gym. The story explained that "Other children will be sitting on chairs in the gym, waiting for the puppet show to start. I will sit with Mama and Mel and Kyle." The next page showed a picture from last year's puppet show and the words, "The lights will be dimmed, everyone will be quiet and the puppet show will begin."

Tomas turned the page. So Manny would know what was expected of him, there was a photo of children watching the show in the dim light, laughing. "I will sit quietly and watch the show. Sometimes the puppets do silly things to make us laugh." Then, "When the show is over, we clap. The lights will go on and I will leave the gym with Mama. We will wave good-bye to the kids and to Papa. Then Mama and I will walk home. Papa will meet us at home after he finishes work."

Tomas didn't know what to say. It was easier to focus on the trivial than on the fact that this new friend had taken the time to make a booklet for his son. "Kyle? Won't Kyle be sitting with his class?" he asked.

"Just this once, it will be all right for Kyle to sit at the side with us. It might make Manny feel more comfortable since this will all be new for him and he might mimic how Kyle behaves. Kids make good models for each other."

"I don't know what to say. Thank you for going to all this work. I'm sorry but we do not know if we should bring Manny or not, but we will think about it."

"Take the book anyway."

Later, Tomas and Maria talked about the puppet show. They hated to deprive their child of anything but what if he behaved badly? Things had been calmer for the most part this past month or so, but not perfect. There had been no *major* incidents of Manny attacking Maria but there were still smaller things like scratching and pinching and throwing things. Plus, Maria had gotten good at dodging

Although neither wanted to distress the other, their minds each replayed scenes from the past - scenes in the grocery store, the doctor's office, the hospital emergency room - all places where life had gone badly awry for their family.

"It's just that he's so unpredictable. I can't always tell when things are going to go badly," said Maria.

"It's been okay at the bakery, though. He's not done anything more there than would any other kid. He even plays all right with Kyle."

"Yeah, that's nice to see."

Maria frowned. "But in the past, I've had some short trips to the supermarket that went all right as well. That's what worries me; I can't guess when things will be fine and when they will be just awful.

"What if he freaked out during the puppet show with all those kids around? What if the people you work with saw how he can be?"

"If the principal saw Manny at his worst, would she think I'm not fit to be around other people's children if I can't even control my own?"

Tomas was still new to his job. What if they brought Manny and he hurt some child? Or even if he turned on his mother? It had become second nature to Tomas to position himself between his son and wife at home just in case Manny attacked her, but at school there were so many children and adults around. What if he wasn't in the right spot to intervene? How could he face these kind people at the school if his son, his own flesh and blood hurt someone? Would he lose his job? It was probably too much to risk.

"Tomas, are they just being nice to you because you're new? We love our son, but why would they want a child like Manny inside their school?"

"I don't know. There seems to be all kinds of children in Madson Elementary School. In the girl's bathroom, there's this area the size of several cubicles put together. There's a change table in there that can be raised and lowered and shelves for diapers and supplies. The girl they use it with is not a baby - she's ten and they change her diapers. There's even a ceiling lift. The EAs use it for a little girl who's in a wheelchair. They told me she has spina bifida. She talks but she can't walk. There's this other boy who wheels around in his chair like a maniac. I even saw him pop a wheelie when he thought no one was watching. What kind of a school allows that?"

The day of the puppet show dawned and Tomas and Maria still had not made their decision when it was time for Tomas to leave for work. "I'll call you at noon to see how things are going, and then we'll decide whether or not you should bring him. All right?"

Manny woke up late, after a restless night. He'd been fitful the evening before, so they skipped his usual bath in favor of just getting him into bed. In the long run, his bedtime was pushed back anyway, and then he was in and out of bed for the next several hours. The neighbors were fighting again and although Tomas and Maria could usually ignore it, Manny seemed particularly affected by the sounds. The fights weren't often, but when they started, Manny was guaranteed a poor night.

Manny's routine was out of whack. He'd woken up too late to have breakfast with his papa. Now he prowled the apartment restlessly, unable to settle to anything. Yearning for a break, Maria watched the clock until Manny's much-loved television show came on. On cue, Manny buried himself under the couch cushions to watch.

Maria gratefully reached for another cup of coffee and a book. She'd have at least twenty minutes of peace.

Not so. While the show usually mesmerized her son for almost a half hour, today he stirred at the first commercial and would not go back to watch, despite all her coaxing and cajoling. He resumed his restless pacing, flicking his fingers at the drapes and lampshades.

"Stop that, Manny. You're going to knock over the lamp."

Crash. Did he do what she'd just warned about on purpose, or was that a coincidence?

As Maria retrieved the broom to clean up the broken shards, Manny's fingers sought other flickering possibilities. He settled on the living room window drapes. At least they won't shatter, thought Maria.

Restlessness drove him on. The day was overcast, so no sun motes came in to entertain him. His travels took him in a circuit around the room, bouncing on his toes as he went. Manny's bare heel found one tiny shard that his mom's broom had overlooked. Small, narrow and sharp, it easily penetrated his skin. He went one step further, and then another before his full weight rested on that heel, driving in the shard.

Maria never knew what caused her son's shriek, but then, she often never knew the reason behind his outbursts. His howl erupted just as she emptied the dustpan into the trash can. Dropping her implements, she ran to her son, but could see nothing attacking him, nothing to account for the ferocity of his yells.

"What, what is it Manny?"

His head was upturned, his hands were flapping, his mouth open in a screech. He jumped up and down on his toes. To calm him, Maria took one hand and tried to guide him to the couch where she hoped to cuddle her son. Manny allowed himself to be led one step, then two, but the third brought his heel once again in contact with the floor. His scream became piercing. In pain, he lashed out. His first blow struck Maria's cheek bone with force that moved her back a step.

With one hand protectively against her cheek, Maria once again came nearer to try to see what was wrong. Putting her face close to get his attention was the wrong move. Manny arched back, but the movement caused his heel to touch down again. Reflexively, his head came forward fast, butting into Maria's nose. Off balance as she was, this blow sent Maria backwards to the floor.

Still, Manny wailed, spinning in circles, hands flapping, hopping on his toes. Maria brought her hand to her face, pulling it away, bloody. While her cheek was likely just bruised, blood gushed from her nose. From experience, she knew that her nose bled freely but this did not necessarily mean it suffered any permanent damage. Still, her head reeled from the pain. Gathering her hands and knees under her, Maria attempted to stand. Her vision spun and for a few seconds she feared she might black out. But, she couldn't. There was no one else here to look after Manny.

Gingerly, she righted herself, and then tried gathering the quivering, fighting mass of nine year old boy into her arms and towards the sofa. It didn't work. He resisted, lashing out blindly. Maria pulled back, trying to regroup. She had to get him to the sofa. Sometimes, he was calmer sinking into the cushions, especially if she threw a heavy quilt over him or even squished him with the extra cushions.

This time, Maria stooped low, trying to come in under his flapping arms, hoping to push him toward the sofa. Only about six feet, she thought. If I can at least get him close, maybe I can pull him the rest of the way, and then drag him up.

Her bear hug attack did get him closer to her goal. Together, they fell backwards. The surprise cut off his shrieks and he caught his breath noisily. Then, Manny's heel dragged on the floor. In panic, he fought in earnest. One hand connected with Maria's sore cheek, the nails dragging down her face to her neck. Usually, she and Tomas waited until Manny was asleep before trying to cut his fingernails. But lately, they must have forgotten. Keeping his nails short was a survival tactic they'd learned after both being scratched innumerable times. Things had been better over the last while, so they'd grown lax. She regretted it now.

He was down on his side with Maria partially on her hands and knees beside him. Now, Manny was angry. An angry Manny usually meant bad news for his mother. His eyes turned toward her, the object that he believed had caused his latest hurt. As Maria rose up on her elbows to approach her son, he lashed out. His forearm connected with the side of her head. Crack. The blow toppled Maria to her side. Manny lay on his back, beating his fists on the floor, wailing. Then his feet got into the action. Unfortunately, he hit his heel in just the wrong spot and the shard pierced in farther.

This time when Maria attempted to approach, Manny again linked his pain with the presence of this other person. His hand fisted where his mama's hair hung over one shoulder. He yanked with all his strength. Maria gave an answering yelp as her body was pulled over top of her son's chest. The added weight stilled Manny momentarily, and then Maria tried to move herself off of her son. Now his other hand reached for a better purchase in her hair.

Maria's, "No, no, no, Manny," had no effect. Her son was beyond reason.

The ringing of the phone startled them both into stillness and silence. The phone rang once, twice, then three times before Manny became accustomed to the sound and launched himself at his mother, all the morning's frustrations coming out in this release of energy.

Maria rolled, trying to protect her face from the onslaught of fury that her son had become. Her initial panic was overtaken by her reasoning powers. The plan. The plan when this happened was for her to get to the bathroom and barricade herself in. The cell phone remained on its charger beside the vanity so that she could call Tomas for help.

Struggling to evade Manny's fists and nails and teeth and flailing legs, Maria edged her way across the floor toward the hall. When she got her torso far enough away, she half crawled, half ran to the bathroom and slammed the door.

Manny the battering ram was right after her. The door opened about two fistfuls wide before Maria got her feet braced against the side of the vanity, the way Tomas had shown her. First, she craned her neck to make sure that none of Manny's body parts poked through the opening. Then she used her leverage to push against Manny's pounding weight and got the door closed. She knew from past experience that just locking the door would do little good. She needed to keep her back and shoulders against the door and her feet flat against the side of the vanity to have enough strength to hold the door shut as her little boy threw his body against the door.

His sobs broke her heart, but she knew that they'd be in even worse trouble if he got to her. He was big enough to do her serious damage. Her greatest fear was that somehow she'd be knocked unconscious in one of these confrontations. Then, what would become of Manny? Anything could happen and he had no sense of danger.

Maria was certain that her son loved her, of course, he did, but when he was in one of these rages, it seemed like he did not even know who she was. All vestiges of the sweet child who cuddled with her were gone. Every motherly instinct in Maria yearned to go comfort her child, take him in her arms and rock him until all the anger and sadness melted away. But, she'd tried that, too many times to count, and the result was never the one she desired. Tomas was clear that she was to keep herself safe, not only for her own sake but for Manny's. The second thing she was to do was to phone Tomas.

Tomas had cobbled together an extra-long piece of wire so that the cell phone charger could remain plugged in at all times and Maria could reach the phone from her protective position against the door. She only had to release one shoulder from its hold to grab the phone and bring it to her.

She reached. Her hand came up empty. She moved one foot from its perch on the vanity long enough to allow her to lift her head to peer at the phone holder. Empty. The phone was not in its assigned place on the charger.

When had they last used it? Its permanent station was here in the bathroom just for such emergencies as this. They *always* left it here.

But the past few weeks had been calmer. They had grown less vigilant because Manny seemed more settled. He'd behaved well in public at the bakery and when out walking with his parents. He'd seemed a happier child and any upsets were mild compared to how things used to be.

How could they become so careless? They'd been lulled into thinking that the worst must be over and let down their guard, no longer checking each morning that the bathroom refuge was all set up, just in case. Now Maria remembered. Her cell was in her purse. She'd put it there the last time she worked at the bakery, so that Tomas could contact her if he and Manny needed anything. She'd forgotten all about it being there and never returned it to the charger. Now it must be dead; she was sure Tomas would have tried that as well as their main phone.

In the other room, the phone rang again, rang ten times without an answer. Maria could picture that phone on the end of the kitchen counter. It would be within easy reach if she was preparing supper. It was one step away for anyone sitting at the kitchen table and only a half dozen paces from the sofa. But from here, barricaded in the bathroom, it was a chasm away.

After only a minute, the ringing started again. Tomas. It must be Tomas trying to reach her. No one else would keep phoning so often. When he received no answer, he would know that there was only one reason Maria did not answer either their land line or her cell phone.

Oh, Tomas. He liked his new job so well. It suited him. He was good at fixing things, liked everything looking nice and he was good with kids. Her Tomas would rush home to save his family, but what if this meant he'd lose this job, too?

CHAPTER SIXTEEN

His toe tapped. Tension was evident in every muscle, every fiber of Tomas' being. Maria would not leave the house on her own with Manny. Even if she thought things were better now and she did venture out with their son, she would take her cell phone. Sure she would, just in case she needed help.

But why didn't she answer? Her cell gave the message that the cellular customer was away from the phone. She always left it on, but maybe she'd forgotten to charge it. That did not explain why she wasn't answering their land line. She knew that he would call by noon; they'd discussed it over breakfast that he'd call and they'd decide if she should bring Manny to the puppet show.

There was only one reason Tomas could think of that Maria would not answer either phone. Because she couldn't.

What of their plan? If Manny had a very bad day and the aggression came out again, Maria was to secure herself in the bathroom where her cell phone lived so she could call Tomas for help.

No answer on either phone and no call for help from Maria was bad, very bad in deed.

Dropping his phone into his pocket, Tomas ran to the office. Dr. Hitkin was just on her way out when she saw Tomas' face.

"Tomas, what is it?"

"It's Maria. My family. I think they're in trouble. I told you...."

"Go, go. Yes, you told me this might happen." She made shooing motions with her hands. "Go. You're needed. Call and let me know how things are."

Stashing his broom in the closet, Tomas thrust his arms into his jacket as he ran. Down the steps of the school, across the grass that he'd just cut that morning and onto the sidewalk. Twelve blocks. Twelve long blocks. Walking to work this past week, those blocks seemed short. In the morning, he was eager to get to work. In the late afternoon, he was anxious to see his wife and son. Now, each block stretched like an endless border, keeping him from protecting those he loved.

It was fine, he told himself. Everything's just fine. Maria and Tomas went to the park and she simply forgot to take her cell phone with her. He'd be home in a few more minutes and find the apartment empty. He'd make a pot of tea and sit down to wait. Soon, he'd hear Maria's laughter coming down the hallway then she and Manny would burst in the door, their cheeks ruddy from the cool air and their hair windblown.

Worst case scenario, Maria would be barricaded in the bathroom with Manny asleep on the hallway floor. Everyone would be safe and sound once they calmed down when he opened the door and walked in. Their plan would work. The only hitch might be the door.

Manny's launches at the door came less frequently now and each one less ferocious than those in his initial frenzy. Maria tried talking to him through the door, keeping her voice low and even and soothing. She reassured him of her love and she longed to open the door and hold him in her arms.

From past experiences, she knew that although every motherly instinct urged her to do just that, it was not a good idea. If she showed herself too soon, before he was sufficiently calm, just her presence could escalate things again and he'd attack.

Her son would attack her. What had she ever done to make her little boy hate her so? When he was like this, he bore no resemblance to the sweet child she held while he slept. She loved the way his long, butterfly lashes lay on his cheeks when he slumbered. He looked so innocent, so gentle, nothing like the enraged child she's witnessed this past half hour.

But his tantrum was winding down. She'd had enough experience with them to know that. Still, it was too soon to venture out, but eventually Manny would sleep, utterly exhausted by all the emotional and physical energy he'd spent.

From the sounds on the other side of the hollow door, Maria could picture the scene. By now, Manny would be on his back, on the floor. The current thumps were from the back of his heels hitting the door as he lay with his hips wedged close to the wall and his legs up against the door. Every so often, he'd give a kick but by now Maria no longer had to exert all her strength to keep the door from bowing in on her.

Gingerly, she got to her feet, using as much stealth as possible so as not to disturb her son and risk his ire starting up again. Soon, it might be safe to open the door a crack and take a peek.

And, soon, Tomas would be home. When he got no answer on either phone, he would surmise what was happening with his family and come home to rescue them. Sad, so sad for a papa to feel he had to stand between his son and his son's mama. Maria knew that it hurt her husband's soul, the things that happened to them in this house. Raising a hand to a loved one was so foreign to Tomas' nature. How had this started with Manny? Where did he get such ideas that it was all right to attack his mama? Tomas gave the example of nothing but respect and gentleness when dealing with their family.

Tomas! How would he get in?

Okay, think, Maria, she said to herself. Think. Did she put the chain on the door when Tomas left for work this morning? Tomas always told her to and it was her habit, but had she remembered this today? Things were out of sync that morning, with Manny sleeping in so late and not joining them for breakfast. Maria remembered sitting at the table after Tomas left, relishing the silence in her home and the indulgence of a third cup of coffee while she read the paper in peace. But, did she get up from the table to engage the chain on the door?

It mattered. It truly did. While Tomas, of course, had a key to their apartment locks, that chain could keep him out. It was an especially stout one, high up beyond Manny's reach, designed to keep their family securely inside and intruders out.

While she strained her ears, listening for the sound of her son's deepening breaths, Maria tried to visualize her morning. No, she could not recall getting up from the comfort of her coffee and going to the door before Manny awoke. No, she had not fastened the deadbolt then.

But later? Oh yes, now she remembered. She was sweeping up the debris from the smashed lamp. With the dust pan balanced in her hands, she walked past the door on her way to the trash bin. Her eye caught the door, noticing the chain swinging from the door frame. She had carefully fed the ceramic lamp remnants into the garbage, then, clutching the dustpan under one arm, fastened the lock.

Oh, dear. Now, there was no way for Tomas to enter the apartment. An integral part of their safety plan was for Maria to make her way to the door, even if she had to keep the kitchen table between herself and her son - even if it meant picking up one of the kitchen chairs and using it to ward Manny off, anything so that she could get to the door and unlock it so that Tomas could come in to help his family.

But, she'd forgotten. Only once before had she not remembered. Now what?

She glanced at her watch, or where her watch should be, but it was gone. A quick glance around the bathroom sink and floor told her that it was not with her. She inspected the long nail scrapes along her forearm, some with drying trails of blood. When Manny scratched her, he must have scraped off her watch.

How long had it been since Tomas's phone calls? Her sense of time was so off when these incidents happened. In the throes of the attacks, they seemed to stretch on for hours, even days, but usually they were no longer than a quarter hour, maybe up to an hour at the worst. But the aftermath, the cool-down part could take varying amounts of time. In truth, Maria had no idea how long it had been since Tomas tried phoning.

But, he'd be here soon. She knew her husband and knew that when she did not pick up the phone, he'd be leaving the school building as quickly as possible and racing home. He'd get home and be stuck out in the hallway, imagining all sorts of dreadful things, like the time she'd had to spend the night in the hospital due to the concussion their son had given her. That was before they'd perfected their plan.

Okay. It had been a while since Manny produced any thumps on the door. Soon, soon now, he'd relax enough to fall into exhausted slumber. Maria knew that once that happened, nothing, not a thing would wake him. It would be safe to sneak by and undo the deadbolt

But, if she left the safety of the bathroom too soon and Manny was still in his aroused state, his rage could return in an instant and he'd be on her. In the close confines of the hall, she'd never be able to get away, or even to drag herself back into the bathroom without slamming the door on any of Manny's body parts.

She needed to time this just right and do it before Tomas got home. If Tomas pounded on the door to be let in, the sound would upset Manny and his anger would elevate into attack mode once again. Then Maria would really be hard pressed to escape from the bathroom refuge to let Tomas in.

It was difficult to gauge the passage of time without her watch, but it had been a while since her son's last desultory thump. She lay down on the floor and pressed her ear to the crack under the door to see if she could hear Manny's breathing. That might give her a clue as to how close to sleep he was, or if mercifully, he was already out. The breath sounds she detected were deep and even.

She stood, looked about the room that had been both her refuge and her prison and took a deep breath. With both hands, she grasped the doorknob, pulling it toward her stomach before turning it. Slowly, ever so slowly, she inched the knob to the right, until the latch cleared the striker. Then, with another deep breath in and out, she held the next one in an attempt to be silent. Maria positioned herself so that her left eye, the good one, the one Manny had not punched, was peeking out the crack of the door.

It felt strange to recognize her apartment when she felt like she'd been in a foreign battlefield for the past half hour. But, there was the broom leaning beside the front door where she'd left it when she turned the deadbolt. Casting her eye down, she saw Manny's jean-clad legs strewn sideways where they'd fallen from their vertical perch on the door. They didn't so much as twitch.

Good. Manny must be asleep. Maria opened the door another inch. Now, her eye and part of one bruised cheek peeked out. She could see her son's torso now and the gentle rise and fall of his chest. Another indication that he was likely asleep. Poor Manny. He needed a blanket and pillow so he could rest more comfortably. She'd get that for him just as soon as she unlocked the door so Tomas could come in.

But now, to get over there. Maria remembered to lift the door slightly on its hinges so that they didn't squeak. Manny hated that sound at the best of times and, so close to his ear, it would surely wake him and send his mood back into the badlands.

Made it so far. The door was not open enough for Maria to slip through. She slipped off her sneakers and tiptoed on sock-clad toes past the twisted legs in the hallway. She stopped, let out her breath and consciously lowered her shoulders and unclenched his fists. Relax. The incident was over now and they'd all be fine.

She continued, gently placing one foot then the other beside Manny's waist, then his shoulders, then by his sweat-plastered head. The hallway didn't allow much room for maneuvering, filled as it was with the sprawled body of a hefty nine year old.

She made it. She was now past her little boy without waking him. She paused to regard his sweet face, serene in sleep. How could this gentle creature turn into a monster bent on harming his mother? What was it that drove her son at such times? Much as she loved him and would give her life for him, it was hard not to resent Manny during the times that he brought such havoc into the lives of his mother and father.

Tomas! That reminded her. She should get that cell phone back on the charger. If only it had been where it was supposed to be, then maybe Tomas would not have had to leave work. She could have kept in touch with him by cell, letting him know when Manny was winding down and that neither of them was seriously hurt.

Now, where had she left it? Likely it remained in her purse, which was beside the bed. Maria turned to head back down the hallway. She'd made it once passed the sleeping Manny, so he should be even more deeply snoozing now. Carefully placing each foot in the angles left by his sprawled body, she made it. Rummaging through her bag, yes she found it. Pressing the button, she saw that it was indeed dead and badly needed to hook up with its charger.

Tiptoeing, Maria made it back to the bathroom, reassured by the tiny click sound of her cell phone making contact with its charging receptacle. Now, to let Tomas in.

Maria grasped the knob of the bathroom door to slide on by just as a frantic pounding started on the door to their apartment. Tomas was there, yelling and pounding to be let in. In her haste to get to her husband, Maria yanked on the bathroom door, causing the hinges to squeal.

Manny stirred, restlessly at first, then with more intent as Tomas's knocks continued. He could hear his dad's voice, even if the words were muffled.

Maria stepped over her son, less cautiously this time, trying to get to the door quickly. But, it was harder to circumvent Manny's body now that it no longer remained inert. He squirmed in that half-sleep, half-awake state of confusion. He bent his knees, resting his feet flat on the floor. Oh, wrong move. Jamming his heel onto the floor brought back a flood of pain and Manny to full consciousness. At his howl, Maria leaned over him in concern.

Another bad move. Manny's eyes opened at the pain to see his mama's nearby face with her glossy hair hanging low within his reach. Every time she came close, he hurt, his senses told him. Rather than trying to get away from him though, his hand reached out and latched onto her hair. His shriek, his pull and Maria's yelp all coincided. The unexpected pull yanked Maria off balance and onto Manny. She attempted to swing her body to the side so as not to crush her son, but was only partly successful. While her head remained at his shoulders, the rest of her body fell onto Manny's legs, her shin flattening Manny's bent leg against the hallway floor. His heel connected with the wall, causing the shard to again dig in.

Manny began rolling from side to side, howling, his fist clenched in Maria's hair. From the hallway came Tomas' yells and pounding, both with his fists and the flat of his hand. Above Manny's shrieks, Maria could hear the desperation in Tomas' voice.

Maria knew she had to do something to get this situation under control. Think, think, she told herself. Logically, she needed to release her hair from her son's grip so that she could cross the apartment to open the door for Tomas. But, how do you extract a sweaty, panicky, little boy fist from multiple strands of long hair? She could cut her hair but there were no scissors within her reach. She could ask him to let go, but knew how effective that would be when Manny was hysterical and beyond reason. She could not remain half crouched with her hair being yanked with each twist of her son's body.

So, she did the only other thing she could think of. Taking a deep breath, she ducked low under his swinging arms, ignoring the painful pull on her hair. With both hands, she grasped under his arms and holding his body tight to hers, raised Manny to a sitting position. She rested there a minute, catching her breath. When had this child gotten so heavy?

But, she was only part way there. With one knee on the floor and the other foot firmly planted, she placed both arms around Manny's body and hoisted him to her and up. Or, that was the plan. They would have both ended up sprawled in a tangle of arms and legs if the hallway had not been so narrow and the wall she fell against held them both up. Rest just for a second, she thought, and then try again. She yelled to Tomas that they were coming, doubtful that he could hear her over Manny's yells and the racket that the man himself created.

Now, another heave with all her might and they were up. Or, rather she was up with Manny leaning heavily against her. At least squeezing him tightly had somehow stopped Manny's tugging on her hair. For the minute, he was limp in her arms, all sweaty, drooling little boy.

Maria gave him a hug and kissed the top of his head. No matter what, he was her son and she loved him.

Next, her plan was to edge them toward the door, that is, unless she could extricate her hair from his grasp. If that was possible, she could cover the distance between here and the kitchen door much more quickly.

Nope, his fingers were wound too tightly around some messy strands to get away without ripping the hair from her scalp. Now that Manny seemed a bit quieter, Maria turned her head to holler to Tomas that they were coming. She hoped he heard.

Keeping one foot braced against the wall, Maria shuffled her other into the hall, towards the kitchen table. Shifting her weight to her forward foot, she pulled Manny's body along, and then brought her rear foot under her shoulders. She took several steps this way, struggling to support Manny, but at this rate, the sun would be up the next day before they made it. Neighbors would have to lend Tomas a blanket and pillow in the hall.

"Manny, Manny, stand up. I can't support you. You have to stand on your own." She gave him a slight shake to get his attention when he didn't respond. "Manny." As he seemed to find his balance, at least partially, she removed her hands from under his armpits and placed them on his shoulders. As she started to rub gently, she felt him tense up, then remembered to instead press down firmly. "Easy, son, it's all right. You're fine. Just relax. Mama's here." She pressed even more firmly to get him off of his toes and flat on his feet.

As Manny rested his weight on his foot, the shard attacked him again. His scream was one of pain and answering volume came from outside in the hallway. Manny's arms flew in the air, flapping wildly.

His hands released the grip on most of his mother's hair, but not all. Some hairs were so entwined between his fingers that they remained glued there. Manny's sudden and rapid flapping caught his mother by surprise and her head was not quick enough to follow his hands. Maria felt the strands tear from her scalp and her scream joined Manny's.

After the initial shock, Maria realized that she was free, free to run to the door. She turned and took off for the kitchen table, intending to round it to reach the door and her husband.

But Manny had other ideas. There she was again, this person who was there every time his foot hurt so badly. He lunged after her. Driven by pain and hysteria, Manny was fast and strong. His hands grabbed the back of his mother's sweater with a jerk, pulling her back off her feet. Maria crashed backwards, into her son, tumbling them both to the ground.

Maria heard the breath rush out of her little boy when she landed on his chest. As swiftly as she could, she rolled off of him, checking to see that he was all right. His panicked eyes stared at her, his mouth moving in an attempt to suck in air. There was no rise and fall to his chest.

He wasn't breathing! What should she do?

Tomas's shouts through the door had been joined by several other voices that had not registered on Maria until now. Tomas was here. Help was here. Surely they'd know what to do for Manny.

CHAPTER SEVENTEEN

Half crawling, half sprinting, Maria lunged the half dozen steps for the door, turning the deadbolt and catching her shoulder on the door as it burst open. She fell into Tomas' arms and his tight squeeze. He held and rocked her for seconds as his eyes scanned the room for their son. "Manny - where is he?"

Then the waiting group heard the harsh indrawn breath as Manny was finally able to suck in air. That first big breath was let out in a howl of fear and rage.

Tomas gave his wife a final squeeze and ran to bend over his son. "Hey, little man. How's my big guy? Papa's home. Are you all right?"

From the other side of Tomas, a heavy blanket appeared and was laid gently over Manny. Then hands, feminine hands, smoothed the blanket over him, to conform to his shape. Sitting back on her heels, Mel smiled a hello.

On the other side of the kitchen, Dr. Hitkin was inspecting Maria's face and head as she handed her tissues for the flood of tears the young mother was producing.

Once she saw that Manny was all right for now, Mel came around the kitchen table to enfold Maria in her arms. Maria remained there, sobbing quietly while Tomas picked up his son, blanket and all and sat with him on the couch. Once again, Manny was becoming drowsy and would soon return to sleep. These episodes left him exhausted.

Maria raised her head. "Mel, what are you doing here?"

Dr. Hitkin stepped forward and held out her hand. "Hi, I'm Delora Hitkin, the principal of Madson School. When Tomas said he had to leave for an emergency at home, I went for my car to see if I could help out."

Maria's questioning eyes turned to Mel. "Dr. Hitkin asked me to be in charge of the school while she left, but when I heard that it was Tomas' family, Rob stepped in and I came along since I know Manny."

"We're a family at Madson and when one of our own is in trouble, we all band together.

"But the puppet show…" asked Maria.

"It's going on right now. I'm sure the kids are having the time of their lives and that next time, Manny will enjoy it as well."

Maria asked, "Don't you have to be there? You're the principal."

"I'd be a poor administrator if I had to be present every second. I have competent staff who will all step forward when needed. The school can get along fine without me for a few hours. Now, let's see to your little boy."

From the couch, Tomas called, "He's asleep now. He seems all right." Carefully, he rose to his feet with his boy in his arms, turned around and deposited him on the couch. "Maria, querida, how are you?"

"I'm fine." Then she remembered her manners. To the others, "Would you like some coffee or tea?"

"Sure, that would be lovely. But, let me make it. Tell me where things are and you sit down," offered Mel. "You've had a rough morning."

With Manny softly snoring on the couch, Tomas righted a fallen chair and straightened the skewed draperies before joining the women at the kitchen table. "The lamp?" he asked his wife.

"Gone. It fell over when Manny's arm hit it."

"I'm sorry." Tomas knew how she had loved that lamp. They'd found it in a flea market shortly after moving into this place. Maria liked the way the etched glass cast shadows.

"Care to tell us what happened?" asked Dr. Hitkin once they were all seated.

Maria looked at Tomas. "I'm not sure. Manny was restless from when he woke up."

"And last night, too," added Tomas. "We had trouble getting him to settle and to go to sleep."

Mel asked, "Was there anything different in his routine? Something that may have upset him?"

"We didn't bathe him last night because he was so off. It was all we could do to get him into his pajamas and into bed. It took him ages to fall asleep, and then he slept in this morning. He's always up in time to have breakfast with us before Tomas leaves for work. Today, by the time he got out of bed, his papa was already gone."

Mel reached into her bag for a piece of paper. "Let's do an ABC."

"A what?"

"ABC stands for antecedent, behavior and consequence. It's a way that we can look at incidents to see if there is a pattern. If we can find patterns, we can sometimes prevent these things from happening again.

"So, under antecedent, or things that happened before, we'll put down these things:

- unsettled evening
- missed his usual bath
- trouble falling asleep
- woke up late
- missed breakfast with his dad
- restless this morning

"Was there anything else? Anything different from how he usually is?" Dr. Hitkin took over while Mel wrote down what Maria said.

"Well, this isn't so different, but he did lots of walking on his toes and flapping. He used his fingers to flick at his ears and he kept shaking his head."

Mel and Dr. Hitkin looked at each other; they'd seen this before. "Has he been sick?"

Neither Maria nor Tomas had noticed anything. Manny hadn't thrown up, he didn't have a runny nose or a fever, but he had been quieter than usual and restless. None of his usual pursuits had interested him for more than a few minutes.

"Let's get back to that in a minute," said Mel. "Now for the behavior part. Maria?"

Maria and Tomas looked at each other. They did not air their dirty laundry in public. Problems at home remained private; they looked after their own. Plus, what would these women think of them if the learned that their son would become violent and attack his mother? What kind of parents could not control their own child? If they thought Tomas was not good with children, might Tomas lose his job?

Watching their hesitation, Dr. Hitkin covered Maria's hand with her own. "You love your boy, we can see that. But you're having some problems with him right now. We understand. Between Mel and me, we have over thirty years of experience with children who have special needs. Will you let us help?"

These were proud people, placing loyalty and self-reliance high at the top of their list of priorities. They were private, sticking to themselves in a culture they were only beginning to understand. But, so far, they had had only good experiences branching out. The people they'd met through the bakery had all been fine individuals. Manny had improved over the past months and had never misbehaved when they were there. So far, Tomas liked his new job. He felt accepted and welcomed by the people at the school. Dare he risk losing that? What would they think of him if they learned the things his son had done? Did these people genuinely want to help and could he dare trust them?

Tomas took a big breath. They had to start somewhere. While protecting his family came first, he had to work to support them. That meant leaving Manny home alone with Maria. He needed them both to be safe. Manny was getting bigger and stronger.

Maria watched her husband's face, understanding the warring within him. She felt the same way. This decision she would leave up to him.

"Manny gets angry," he began. "It's unpredictable; we never know when it might happen. Sometimes it happens when we are both here, but most often it is when he is just with his mama." He put his arm around Maria's shoulders. "A child could not ask for a better mother than my wife. We do not understand how he can turn on her like this." He brushed aside Maria's hair and ran a gentle finger down her bruised cheek. "Once, our Manny lashed out and broke his mother's nose. We had to go to the emergency room."

Tears overflowed Maria's eyes. "I do not think he means to hurt me. At other times, he is affectionate and we play together. But something comes over him sometimes and he becomes a different child. When he was smaller, I could just hold him in my arms until the worst had passed. But now that he is bigger, he is so strong when he is angry."

"I understand," Mel told her.

"But you have never seen Manny when he is like this."

"True, but I have seen other children, including our son, Kyle."

"Kyle? Surely not."

"No, it has not happened in a long time, but when he first came to live with Ben, it was common. We had a few incidents when he was in my kindergarten class."

"At school?" Maria could not imagine such as thing.

"We're prepared and have enough people around to help and to keep everyone safe. And, the more time we spend with the child, the better we get at reading him and hopefully heading things off before they get this far."

Maria confessed, "We try to be good parents."

"Of course, you do. And for a typical child, you would likely be perfect parents. But some children are just more difficult to raise and the usual things may not be enough. Parents of kids with special needs may need to learn more strategies and have a wider bag of tricks at their disposal."

"What do you mean by strategies?"

"Some things are simple," Mel explained. "Like the social stories we used with Manny at the bakery. Things like this help prepare a youngsters for what will happen and what will be expected of him. Then there are other strategies that can help calm the child, like pressing firmly on his shoulders, holding him snuggly, and using things like a weighted blanket." She pointed at where Manny lay sleeping on the couch.

Maria got up to inspect the blanket. "It is quite heavy. We just had a light sheet over him last night because he seemed so restless."

Mel directed them back to her sheet of paper. "Let's look at the C column now for consequences." She turned to Tomas. "You mentioned that this happens when you're home too, but maybe not as severely. Tell me, what do you do after Manny gets upset and things start to escalate?"

"I'm bigger and stronger than Maria, so I can hold him. I pick Manny up, bring him to that couch and hold him tightly with my arms around him. Maria brings us a blanket and fits it snuggly around us and I just hold on tight until I can feel him start to relax. Maria sits close by and strokes his hair. Sometimes she sings to him. It might take a while but he calms down and sometimes falls asleep."

"Ah," Dr. Hitkin observed. "You're applying pressure with your hug - a good strategy. That's the same principle behind using a weighted blanket. Weight and pressure can have a calming effect."

Mel continued. "So, a consequence that Manny receives is a deep pressure hug from his dad. That would help settle him. It also may be a sensation he's craving and he's learned that if he raises a fuss, someone will give it to him."

Tomas had not considered this. "But he goes to such extremes, especially with his mother."

"Did Maria used to provide such tight hugs when he was upset?"

"When he was smaller, yes, I used to," admitted Maria. "But I can't now."

"I wonder if he's trying to get that deep pressure hug and when you don't supply it, he ups the ante to get you to respond in the way he wants, the way he always used to. When you don't, he must get frustrated."

"Does he ever."

Dr. Hitkin asked, "Would it be all right with you if we tried to come up with other ways for Manny to get what he might feel he needs?"

"At this point, we'll do anything," said Tomas.

"To start with, I have a weighted blanket at home that you can try. Kyle doesn't use it anymore."

"You'd do that for us? Thank you," said Tomas.

Mel continued. "It's tough for kids who are nonverbal. They can't tell us what they want or need, so we have to become keen detectives, watching their behavior and using trial and error.

"It's frustrating not to be able to make your basic wants and needs known. The child may be trying to communicate, but we don't understand. Can you imagine how you'd feel in that position? How angry you might become? I'm not excusing what Manny has done and no one has the right to hurt another person. But there is something behind his behavior. It's our job to figure out what."

It was Dr. Hitkin's turn. "One of the first things we like to do is check if there is a physical reason behind the negative behavior. You'd be surprised how often we learn that a child has a bladder infection or a sinus or ear infection that we could not discern, but made the child feel restless and grouchy. While other kids might tell their parents that they have a headache or a stomachache or their ear hurts, kids who are nonverbal don't have that luxury."

Maria's eyes met those of her husband. Was it possible that their child was sick or in pain and they didn't know it?

"When was his last medical checkup?"

Neither Tomas nor Maria could remember. They only took him when he was sick, which rarely happened. Besides, visits to the doctor were expensive.

"You're aware that you now have medical benefits, don't you? That's part of your contract with us."

"We had no benefits at my last job. Do these benefits cover all of my family?"

"There are limits, like with any plan package, but yes, if you take Manny to the doctor, the cost of the visit and basic procedures are all covered. Your health card may not have arrived in the mail yet, but we'll have your policy number at the office. As long as you have that, you'll be covered."

"I think it's worth taking him to the doctor," Mel said. "The fact that he was restless last night and this morning may indicate that he's not feeling well. You said that he was flicking at his ears and shaking his head. There's a possibility that he could have an ear infection or something else. Having an infection can alter a child's behavior, making him irritable and out of sorts. For some kids, their frustration with this may lead to aggression, especially when he has no way of letting you know what is wrong."

Maria said, "There's a clinic just a few blocks over. Maybe we could take him when he wakes up."

Mel had another thought. "Before you go, you might want to stop by my house to pick up that weighted blanket Kyle used to use. Doctors' offices can smell funny to some kids and they don't like it. They have to get up on this high, narrow table which can be scary if they think they might fall off. Then, this strange person starts touching them and using instruments like the stethoscope or a tongue depressor, sticking things in their mouth and nose and ears. This stranger will want the kid's clothing removed and it can be chilly. All these things can be upsetting and you don't know how Manny will react."

Tomas was ready to back out of the whole thing. They'd just gotten Manny calmed.

"It'll be okay," Mel assured him. "There are some things you can do to help. Take along the weighted blanket and use it both while you're in the waiting room and during the examination. Only remove as much clothing as you need to for the doctor to examine that part of his body at a time. Keep the weighted blanket on. For part of the exam, you can hold Manny on your lap, hugging him tightly."

Somewhat reassured, Maria nodded.

"And, if you stop by our house, I'll give you a story that I made for Kyle about going for a check-up at the doctor's office. No guarantees, but it might help.

"You know, if you used the same doctor, the pictures would even be accurate. And, Dr. Finley understands kids with autism. His office is across from the park. Here, if you have a phone book, I'll get the number for you."

"But Manny doesn't have autism."

Dr. Hitkin and Mel looked at Tomas without comment.

Mel stood. "Anyway, here's my address. Millie, our housekeeper is there now and she knows where this stuff is. I'll give her a call to let her know that you're coming by. The doctor story is in a green binder. There are lots of stories in it, but look on the tabs for the one that says doctor. We keep a bunch of stories for when they're needed. If you find that this one helps Manny, I'll make a photocopy for you."

As they left, Dr. Hitkin told Maria, "And you might want to get yourself checked out, too. That's a nasty bruise you have."

Mel poked her head back in the door. "When you pick up the blanket and story, you might consider telling Manny that this is where Kyle lives and that on the weekend, he could come over to play."

CHAPTER EIGHTEEN

Maria shut the door and leaned her back on it. "Did I hear that right? Was Mel actually inviting Manny over to play with her son after she heard the things he can do?"

"That's what it sounded like to me. But let's see how this doctor thing goes first."

While Manny slept, Tomas called the number Mel had given him. He explained the problem and that they wondered about an infection. The answering receptionist asked if Manny was complaining. Uncomfortably, Tomas admitted that his son did not speak.

"That's all right. We have several patients here who have autism and other developmental disabilities. With kids, we don't like to leave suspected ear infections too long. Come on in around three o'clock."

They started getting Manny ready as soon as he stirred. He wasn't interested in lunch, despite their coaxing. Usually, he had a healthy appetite, even if he did insist on sticking to his few, chosen foods.

Then, he needed a bath. That sweaty boy smell was something only a parent could love. Manny's diaper and clothes needed changing before they could leave.

Checking the slip of paper in her hand, Maria confirmed that this old, two-storey Victorian house matched the address Mel had given. While Tomas waited in the car with Manny, she rang the ancient door bell. Its distinctive peals were audible through the heavy, lead glass door.

Soon, an older woman opened the door. "You must be Maria. I'm Millie. Is Manny in the car?" She peered past Maria, spotted Tomas and

Manny and waved. "I look forward to meeting him. Mel said that you might bring him over to play with Kyle on the weekend."

"Um, well, we'll see. Manny has a doctor's appointment this afternoon and we want to see how he is first." She accepted the laminated papers from Millie and thanked her.

On the way to the doctor's office, Maria sat in the back of the car with Manny and read him the story, over and over. Although his parents were getting tired of it, once his focus turned to the pages, his attention did not waver. Self-consciously, Maria went over it again in the waiting room. There was only time for one repetition though, because the nurse came to put them in an examining room almost immediately. She explained that she knew kids with autism found the waiting room difficult and he'd be calmer during the examination if he had time to become accustomed to the room and the examine table first. She bustled away before Tomas could explain that his son was not autistic.

They only had time to reread the story twice more before a tap on the door signaled that the doctor had arrived. He introduced himself, shaking hands with first Tomas, then Maria and squatting down to greet Manny. He did not seem put off by the little boy's wandering gaze. Firmly, he reached for Manny's right arm, placed the child's hand in his own, larger one and gave a firm squeeze.

"He has to get used to me touching him," he explained to the parents. Then, he asked Tomas to sit up on the examining table, ignoring his protest that he was not the patient. He reached for his otoscope, inserting a fresh probe. He showed it to Manny and asked him to watch while he looked in his dad's ears. Then, it was Maria's turn to have her ears checked, but this time, he asked Tomas to lift Manny onto the table beside his mom so that Manny could have a look as well.

Next, the doctor asked the parents to each sit on either side of Manny on the table, sandwiching him in closely. His hope was that this would make the child feel more secure and that with parental arms around him, he was in no danger of slipping off the table. "Squeeze him in nice and tight," the parents were instructed.

After looking in Manny's ears, nose and throat, the pronouncement was made. "Your son has acute otitis media with effusion. That means he has an infection in his middle ear. His ear drum is red and slightly bulging. Have you noticed Manny pulling at his ear or flicking them or shaking his head?"

When the physician learned that it had been years since Manny had a physical examination, he started in right away. "We need to check for other signs of infection as well." As Manny lay on the table, his mom covered him with the weighted blanket, glancing nervously at the doctor.

He nodded. "Good idea. We'll only undress him as much as we have to. While I examine him, do you think you can distract him?"

Maria picked up the story and began reading. As she started, the doctor looked over and smiled but waiting until she'd finished to comment. "I recognize that. Is Mel your son's teacher?"

"No, we're just friends. She loaned us this story for this afternoon's visit."

"You're lucky to have her as a friend. She knows a lot about autism. Madson's a great school for kids with special needs."

The doctor warmed his hands before the examination, working his way down Manny's body quickly but thoroughly. He knew he had limited time. "His lungs sound clear. The infections seems confined to his ears and sinuses. This is likely a hold-over from that cold you said he had a month or so ago."

He held up Manny's arm and said to him, "Watch. I'll show you a trick. I bet I can make your arm jump." He tested the reflexes in each elbow and was rewarded by a tiny giggle. Next, he bent Manny's knees up and tested the reflexes there. "Do you think your foot will bonk your daddy?"

The next reflex to assess was the one of the sole of his foot. As he lifted the first foot, Manny flinched and pulled away. The doctor paused and moved on to the other foot. No flinching there. He squatted down to take a look at the sole of Manny's foot without touching it. "Ah, ha." He called Maria over and pointed. "See that area there? Look by his heel. There's that area of redness with a lighter part in the center. Wait until I get my light." He shone a bright, magnifying light on the spot and the splinter came into view, the thin shard glittering reflected light. "That has to come out. It looks pretty sore."

"How do we do that?" Maria was frightened for her son and for how he'd react to any procedure.

"Simple. This is not a big deal." First, he gently swabbed the area with a non-stinging disinfectant and blew on it to dry it. Manny gave a laugh and moved his foot. "Tickles, eh?" Next a numbing substance was sprayed to dull the sensations on his skin. "I want to freeze the area in case I have to probe deeper to extract whatever is in there. Then I want to thoroughly cleanse the area to prevent infection. If I numb the area first, then Manny won't feel when I insert the needle to freeze the area."

While Tomas kept his son amused by reading a children's book, the doctor froze the area. He explained that he'd give it time to take effect, and then be back in a few minutes.

When he returned he tested the effectiveness of the freezing by running a pin alongside the splinter. The child never moved. Maria watched as the doctor made a small incision with a scalpel, then used long tweezer-like things to probe the open wound until he found the splinter and removed it. Using the magnifying light, he inspected the area but didn't see anything else. The cut was so small it didn't require any stitches. Instead, more antiseptic went on, then a butterfly bandage. Soft cotton was the next layer, with a larger bandage over that. "This should make it easier for him to walk on it, but I think he'll have much less discomfort now that that sharp little piece is out of there. It must have dug in at every step. No wonder he walked on his toes when he came in here today."

Neither Maria nor Tomas mentioned that their son frequently toe-walked, but they had both noticed how often he did it this afternoon.

"Between a splinter and an ear infection, this young man's had a rough day," the doctor continued. "By the way, for our records, when and where was your son diagnosed?"

"Diagnosed?"

"Who first told you that he has autism?"

"Autism? But, he doesn't. No one has ever diagnosed him with anything."

"And why is that?" the physician wanted to know.

Flustered, Tomas said, "Well, no one ever has. Manny stays home with us and we look after him."

"Do you mean he doesn't go to school?"

"Sir, our son is not like other children. You noticed that he still wears diapers. He can't learn."

"Whoa. I don't think you'd want to let your friend Mel hear you say that. She'd take a strip off you. All kids can learn. They might do it at their own pace and maybe learn different things, but they can learn."

As Dr. Finley wrote a prescription for an antibiotic, he urged Tomas and Maria to get Manny in school. Mel was a good person to talk to about it. "He really should be in school. You'll be surprised at the progress you'll see in him. And, take this with you as well. I'm making a referral to a developmental pediatrician. My guess is that this is an autism spectrum disorder but I'm not a specialist in this area. You need to know what you're dealing with so that you can find the right strategies and therapies that will help your son be all that he can be."

Then, he took Maria's chin in his fingers to inspect the injuries to her face.

Thankfully, Manny approved of the taste and texture of the liquid antibiotic and gulped his spoonful without complaint. He was subdued for the rest of the day, complying with his parents' requests to eat a bit of supper then get ready for his bath. Tomas taped a plastic bag around the sore foot so it would not get wet. With his back against the corner of the tub and his foot resting on the tub's top edge, Manny sat slumped, relaxing in the warm water until he became drowsy. He was asleep by the time he was dried off, pajama-clad and tucked tightly into bed.

He wasn't the only exhausted one in the family. Both his parents had spent too much emotional energy, plus Maria was sore from her confrontation with Manny that morning. A lot had happened that day.

"Tomas, what did you think about your boss and Mel coming here this morning?"

"I don't know what to think. At first I was embarrassed to have someone else see the problems we have in our family. I still feel that way, but they didn't make me feel ashamed. I'm not sure they understand just how awful things can get, but they had a glimpse. And, they saw your poor face."

"Somehow, I didn't feel quite so alone with them here, like there were other people on our side. Dr. Hitkin didn't accuse us of being awful parents. Instead, she tried to help."

"And, they weren't scared off. Can you believe that Mel still mentioned Manny coming to play with her son?"

When they were in bed, before drifting off to sleep, Tomas mused about Madson School. "You should see it, Maria. There are kids there with disabilities - kids who don't walk, kids who don't talk, and even a couple who remind me of Manny."

"Like Manny? But he can't learn like other kids."

"Maybe not, but I don't think he's any worse off than these other kids I saw there. And everyone seems to think it's normal that they're in school."

"What would they learn?"

"I don't know. I don't see them carrying books, but they're in the classrooms. They seem to move around a lot, sometimes in one room, then in another."

"They have these other people there too, people who aren't teachers but sort of like helpers. They work with these kids or sometimes with the class while the teacher does things with the special needs kids."

"You said that Dr. Hitkin asked why Manny was not in school, even though she knows that he's different."

"Yeah, she's mentioned it a couple of times. And when she invited him to the puppet show, she called it 'a start'."

Tomas thought that Maria had fallen asleep when she asked, "Do you think it's possible that Manny could go to school?"

CHAPTER NINETEEN

After considerable debate, Maria and Tomas decided to brave taking Manny to the bakery Saturday morning. Maybe the antibiotic was taking effect or maybe their son was just ebbing into another up cycle where life would run more smoothly for a while. Regardless of the reason, they thought they should take advantage of the relative peace and get out of the house, their first venture since that bad, bad day.

Ellie met them at the door and followed her usual routine with Manny. They took up right where they left off as if the stressful week had not occurred. If Ellie knew that things had been rough for Manny, she didn't let on.

As Manny munched his gingerbread man, his parents began to relax. Maybe this would be all right. This place had become almost a sanctuary for them, a public refuge where they could go when they'd been cooped up too long inside, and a place where they and their son seemed accepted.

Maria glanced around uneasily as the bakery started filling up. She watched Ellie's practiced speed, greeting customers, serving orders and clearing tables. Should she help? Ellie hadn't asked her to and really, she should not leave Tomas and Manny alone.

Tomas' shoulders stiffened. He couldn't help it. Maria turned toward Tomas' gaze and heard Ellie's, "Hey Munchkin," signaling the arrival of her nephew, Kyle. Maria turned away from the door. Like Tomas, she was embarrassed to see Mel, this woman who now knew the shame of their family problem. How would Mel react?

Soon, Maria had her answer.

"Mind if we join you?" Ben asked. Without actually waiting for the okay from either Tomas or Maria, he lifted another table over to join theirs, sat down and hooked two chairs with is foot to drag them to the double table for his wife and son. He nodded to the counter. "They'll be forever there with Ellie, discussing the merits of all the choices, and then Kyle will end up with the same thing he always chooses." He nodded at Manny's plate. "Hmm. I see a pattern here."

"Hey, Manny." Mel knelt beside Manny's chair with her hand raised. And waited. And waited. He needed more of a cue. "It's been a while, hasn't it? Can you give me a high five?" One, two, three, four, five, six seconds passed, then Manny raised his hand to slap Mel's, possibly with more force than necessary but it was hard to grade your movement without looking directly at the target. Still, Manny was unerringly accurate considering he gave Mel no more than a sideways glance. "Look, here comes Kyle. Kyle, come greet your friend."

With both hands clutching his cookie-bearing plate, Kyle carefully deposited his cargo on the table, then joined his step-mom beside Manny. A little shy, he leaned into Mel, looked at Manny's legs and said a barely audible, "Hi."

Manny gave no sign that he'd heard and made no noise. Fearing that his child was being rude to these nice people, Tomas opened his mouth to prompt his son. Before a word came out, he watched Manny raise his hand in the air to Kyle. Kyle knew the drill and high fived the other boy. Mel squeezed a shoulder of each boy, and then sat down, as if this was an everyday occurrence.

The boys ate silently while the adults chatted. The awkwardness Tomas and Maria had feared didn't happen and they began to relax. When both boys had thoroughly dismantled their gingerbread men, Mel guided the kids to the play area in the corner. Maria gave her permission reluctantly, scared of what might happen. Mel invited her to join her at a table beside the boys, with a reassuring, "It'll be all right. We'll stay by them and watch, but I'm sure they'll be fine."

She was right and the boys resumed the game they'd played the week before of tower building/tower destroying.

"Wouldn't you think they'd get tired of doing the same thing over and over?" asked Maria.

"You don't know Kyle well if you'd say that. He can repeat something over and over if he's intent on the game. But we don't let things go on too long because he can stim on it."

"Stim?"

"Yeah, he can get too involved in a repetitive action, doing the same thing over and over and over. Sometimes it gives him comfort, but we're careful. If this game goes on too long, I'll play with them and try to change if up a little. It's good for Kyle to learn to be flexible and that there's more than one way of doing something. He may not like it, especially at first, but over the years we've expanded his repertoire of play by doing this."

"Manny likes to do the same things all the time, too. Like he flicks our living room drapes. Or, he plays with his hands in the sun beam coming through the window. He can stack blocks for hours, too."

"Hmm. Do you think it's good for him?"

Maria sat back in her chair. "I never really thought about it. It's just something he does. And when he's doing those things, he's quiet. Sometimes I really appreciate that quiet."

"No kidding. I know what you mean. It's good to give kids with autism time to themselves; sometimes they need to just veg out and relax because often things are tough for them. There's a fine line between adequate time to do exactly what they want and getting too caught up in repetitive actions. It's hard to find that fine line, isn't it?"

Maria was puzzled. "We've always just thought that this was Manny. And, autism. His doctor mentioned that word, too. But Manny doesn't have autism. I've heard of kids with autism and they sit in the corner and rock and bang their heads and are in their own little world. That's not Manny. I saw that old movie, *Rainman* too and that's not Manny either."

"You're right that some kids with autism are like Dustin Hoffman's character in *Rainman*, but that's rare and there are some kids so affected by the autism symptoms that may seem locked in a world of their own, but again, that's rare and might be only for a portion of that child's life. We know so much more about autism these days and how to help kids regulate their emotional state and learn."

Hesitatingly, Maria said, "Manny's doctor is making a referral to a developmental pediatrician for us. He thinks we should find out if Manny does have autism." She stared at her son before raising her eyes to this friend. "And, he said that Manny should be in school."

"He's right," agreed Mel. "He should be in school."

"But you've seen how he can be! Well, you didn't actually see it, but you heard us talk about it and you saw my bruises. He can hardly be around other children."

Mel regarded the boys and the mixture of their giggles as yet another tower collapsed in a mess of blocks. She looked at Maria. "He's around my son."

"Yes, but you're here and I'm here."

"True, but are we interfering in their play?"

Maria tried a different track. "Manny's different. He can't learn like other children."

"Nope, he probably can't. Neither does Kyle. Kyle certainly learns but his learning style is different than that of some of the other kids in his class. In fact, most of us learn differently."

Maria shook her head. "You know what I mean. Obviously something is wrong with my son. He doesn't talk, no matter how much I've tried to make him. Have you ever heard of a nine year old who does not talk? And he's still in diapers. No school would want a child like that."

"I would. Madson School would. I can guarantee you that Manny is welcome at our school. He would be well taken care of and once he's been there for a while, he'll learn and grow and you'll be surprised at the changes in him."

"He's so big. I've seen kids walking to school, kids who look like they're in kindergarten. What would happen if Manny was in with them and he got mad? He could seriously hurt those little kids."

"He wouldn't be in with the five year olds. If you bring him to school, he'll be with kids his age or close to his age."

"How could that be? He doesn't read or write. I know what other nine year olds do and Manny would not fit in."

"No, not right now. He's not ready to sit at a desk and work on math problems. But we don't know just what he *can* do. We have kids in all our classes who are not doing grade level work but who benefit from spending some time with children their age. Kids are good role models for each other. You'd be surprised how much they watch each other and model their actions on what they see going on around them."

"That's just it. Manny pays little attention to anyone around him." She watched the boys and amended, "Except for maybe Kyle. Look, he's watching Kyle and waiting for him to run the car into the blocks."

Mel nodded. "That's what I mean about kids being good for each other. Remember the first time my little hellion of a son ruined Manny's tower? There was always the chance that Manny would get mad, but he looked at Kyle, saw Kyle laughing and that made him think. Now, the kids are actually playing together."

"Just say that Manny could go to school. I mean, I love my son, but I am aware of his limitations. What would he learn?"

"I don't know what he'll learn down the road; I don't think anyone can predict that. But for now, we'd start with basics. I like to start where kids are, look at them from a developmental viewpoint and go from there." At Maria's quizzical look, she explained. "By developmental, I mean the stage of development he's at and that will vary. Take play, for instance. Small children go through a stage where they are solitary in their play. Then, as they mature, they may play alongside another child, but not really play *with* the other kid. Then they develop the skills to actually play together." She nodded at their boys. "It looks like Manny's entering that phase now."

"As nice as it is to see Manny playing with another boy, his play is not really what concerns us. There are other things that are priorities for us.

117

Things that will help him in life."

"Play is the primary way young children learn. While Manny's playing, he's learning all sorts of things. If you watch, he's learning patience. He has to wait until Kyle does his part in breaking down the tower. And, Kyle must wait for Manny to rebuild the tower. They're also learning turn-taking. Both are important skills in life."

"I hadn't thought about the wait part. Manny is *not* good with waiting; when he wants something, he wants it right now. Learning to wait would be a good thing. What else would he learn in school?"

"While we're still on play, he'd learn that other people have ideas and wants that differ from his. He may not like it, but sometimes he'd get his way and sometimes he'd need to follow someone else's lead, just like he did the first time Kyle smashed up the tower he was building. Manny compromised, another good skill to have.

"In order to compromise and follow someone else's ideas, you have to watch. Play is one of the ways that kids learn to read the body language that other people give off and to understand those non-spoken signals. He'll learn how to have fun with others and that being in the company of other people is pleasurable."

"He's always been pretty solitary, only letting Tomas or I play with him in a limited way. We try, but he seems to prefer his own company much of the time."

"There's nothing wrong with that to a certain extent, but too much time alone does not allow him the opportunities to gain social and coping skills."

"And, in school....?" Maria asked.

"He'd have more opportunities to learn how to tolerate other people. No matter who we are, or where we are, life is a group affair and we have to be able to rub shoulders with other people, even when we don't feel like it. Sometimes others annoy us or we just want to be left alone, but we can't be by ourselves. We need to learn coping skills for those times and how to tolerate the presence of others."

"That makes sense but those aren't the things I think about when I consider school. No one taught me stuff like that when I was in school, but that was in another country. It must be different here."

"No, likely it's not that different. These things are all part of what's called the 'hidden curriculum', important parts of school that are not taught. Most kids pick this stuff up automatically on their own, but with some children, we need to explicitly teach these things.

They watched the demolition of yet another tower. Then, Mel continued. "These are things like how to follow along in a group. How to share a laugh with other people, when to wait and when to forge ahead."

"And, you think Manny could learn these things in school? Couldn't we just teach them at home?"

"It's possible," Mel admitted. "But, has he learned them so far?" She paused. "I didn't mean that to sound unkind. It's just that these things while not impossible are tough to teach at home with one child. Lots of this learning lends itself to group situations more than when a child is alone or with just one adult."

"I don't know. I get what you're saying and these things would help Manny, but he's so different than other kids his age. I see them walking down the street and much as I'd wish it were otherwise, I can't see him joining them."

Mel reached over and squeezed Maria's hand. "No, not right now he can't. He's not ready. But who knows what is in his future?"

The two women watched their sons who did not seem to tire of playing the same game over and over again. Mel continued. "Manny does not have to be just like other kids to be around other kids. At Madson School, we have kids of all skills and abilities and there's a place for each and every one."

Maria turned and put her elbows on the table. "Tell me exactly what Manny would do in school. I can hardly see him sitting still for a history lesson."

"That depends on the lesson. If it's a lecture, no, he would not like it. Too many words and terminology would make it hard for him to relate to and to pay attention. But some lessons are more hands-on and he may be able to participate on some level. He may not get out of the lesson each and every point that some kids would soak in, but he could still benefit from the exposure and the activity and being with his peers."

"When Manny gets bored or restless or upset, bad things happen. You saw the after-math of one episode, but I'm ashamed to say that it happens more often than we'd like." She rethought what she'd said. "Actually, we'd prefer that they never happen but that seems to be out of our control." She raised her chin and looked Mel directly in the eyes. "I've been hurt by our son, hurt enough to go to the hospital. I'm a lot bigger and stronger than school children are. I could not live with myself if our son hurt a child. That is a big reason to keep him out of your school or any other school. He could hurt someone."

"Yep, that is a possibility."

Maria had been so hoping that Mel would not agree with her. Her shoulders slumped. "So I guess we should continue on as we have been."

"Not necessarily," Mel told her. "I don't want to paint a picture for you that things will be all rosy at school. Just the opposite may happen. This would be a big change for Manny and the initial period of adjustment can be rough.

"But, I'm confident that he'll come through it - we'll all come through it, and things will get better after that. Look, if he stays home the way he has been, he'll likely continue down the same path he's headed now. He's getting bigger and stronger. When he's frustrated, the chances of hurting someone are high and that someone is likely you. It's not just you I'm worried about, but what if you fall in a skirmish and knock yourself out? What would happen to Manny then?"

"That's what Tomas worries about, too."

"I don't see things changing a lot for the better if Manny continues to remain at home. But, if he's in school, we have a greater chance of teaching him other ways to manage his frustrations."

Maria sort of agreed. "Maybe."

"Another thought. Sometimes kids act out because they're bored. Being in the same apartment day after day, with the same toys could get boring. Just like we need to get out every so often, so do kids, even kids with special needs. They get bored, too. He would be less bored at school because there are more people around, more going on and he'd be learning new skills."

"I don't really think of Manny as being bored, but possibly he is. It's hard to know when he can't tell us."

"That's another thing we'd work on at school," said Mel. "A communication system. Sometimes kids get aggressive when they're frustrated because they can't make some need or want known. Can you imagine what it must be liked to want something, really want it, but be unable to convey that to the very people who could help you?"

"We've seen that with Manny. Like when he wants something to eat and we can't figure out what it is he wants. He's torn cupboards apart looking for something that we're probably out of, but we can't figure out what it is he's after. If we knew, we'd run out and buy it, but we just don't know. He gets so worked up and mad."

Mel nodded. "It must be awful for him. But, there are things that could help."

"You mean you'll teach him to talk?"

"That, of course, is the ultimate goal and the easiest form of communication. Some kids who are on the autism spectrum come to spoken language later than other kids. Some may develop a limited vocabulary, some will eventually speak as well as their peers, while some may never acquire the skills to speak."

Maria slumped. More discouraging news.

Mel held up a finger. "Wait. Even if the latter is the case for your son, there are other ways he can communicate. Some kids use dedicated communication devices, or iPad apps. Others use a simple picture system. We would likely start with a few pictures for Manny, and then build up from there. We would experiment to see which system he takes to.

"You should see the look on a child's face when they first make the connection that by giving someone a picture of something, they actually receive that thing that they want. What power! Kids just blossom. Suddenly they have control. If they give their mom a picture of orange juice, then they get a glass of juice. No whining, no tantrums, just a simple pointing to a picture then presto, they get what they want."

CHAPTER TWENTY

Dr. Hitkin stopped Tomas in the hallway. "Does Manny eat pizza?"
"Yes, certainly. Why?"
"This Friday is pizza day at our school. I thought Manny might like to join us for lunch. Maria, too of course."
Tomas went with his reflex response. "I don't think so. Manny's not a group kind of kid and he's never been in a school before." He picked up his mop. "But, thank you very much all the same." He moved toward the outside doors to remove the evidence of hundreds of dusty little foot prints in the entryway.

Dr. Hitkin moved along with him. "This might be a nice introduction to school for him. He could come a bit early to see where his dad works. He and Maria could sit with Kyle and Mel to eat. I hear that those boys get along well."

"Yes, they have played together at the bakery." Tomas paused, unsure if he should say more. But his fatherly pride would not let him hold it in. He beamed. "You should see my boy. He plays, actually plays with Kyle, playing little kid games and he giggled! We had almost given up hope of seeing such a thing."

"I understand how you feel. I hear that from a lot of parents as their children acquire new skills. This is just the start for your son. Wait until you see the progress when he's around other kids every day."

Tomas closed off again. "My Maria and I, we have not made any decisions about that yet. It is a big step." And, what would happen if Manny got angry here? He could hurt someone. Would they blame it on Tomas and he'd lose his job? He did not dare voice that worry to his boss. "We are waiting to hear what the doctors have to say about the assessment."

"No matter what the assessment results are, Manny is welcome here as a student and if he just wants to come have some pizza with us on Friday." She started to walk away, then turned back. "You might want to stop by Mel's room. She said she had something to give you for Manny."

When Tomas entered the apartment, Maria was at the table, papers spread around her, a frown on her face.

In Tomas' experience, important-looking papers were not good news. "What is it? Are we being evicted? The rent's up to date but have too many people complained about Manny's noises?"

Maria rubbed the side of her husband's face. "No, it's nothing like that. Our home's safe. The assessment report on Manny came today but I can't understand what it says. Look, there's eight pages, all about Manny, but the words...."

Tomas sat down to start reading. He opened the drawer that held his reading glasses, hoping that would help. He got some words, the smaller ones, but there were too many foreign terms. Since English was a second language for both of them, they assumed the fault was with them.

"Do you think we should make an appointment with the doctor to ask him to tell us what all this means?"

"Doctor appointments cost money. Our insurance only covers so many a year. But I'm having trouble getting past the second page here. Look at the words they use - 'pervasive developmental disorder'. I get the last one, even if I don't like them using it to refer to my son. But the rest?"

"I wonder, Tomas, what about Mel? Do you think we could ask her to take a look at this letter? She's a teacher, I think some special kind of teacher."

"This letter probably says things about us, about our family and our son. And, it might not be good. Do we want to jeopardize her friendship by having her read this?"

"She's already seen us at our worst and still talks to us. Ben, too. He didn't see the things Manny did, but he likely heard about it."

"We have to trust someone and I'm not sure who else to turn to for help."

While Ben sat with the boys as they played in the corner, Maria, Tomas and Mel huddled over the report. As soon as Mel saw the thick sheaf of papers, she sighed. "I see why you were having difficulties. They often write these reports in jargon." As she peered at the first page, she muttered, "Why can't they use plain language?"

"Okay," she continued. "Here's how you tackle these things. See the first paragraph here? That usually says why the patient was referred, his age, height, and stuff like that. These next pages talk about the various tests they used during the assessment, and then they go on to talk about how he performed on each measure and how they drew their conclusions. It's interesting, but might not mean as much to you just yet. You probably want to know the bottom line.

"When I'm in a hurry, I just read the opening bit, then flip to the back." She thumbed through the pages. "Here. See where it says summary? This is where the good part starts." She read silently to herself, her finger skimming across the lines. "Yep," she said.

Two anxious faces peered at her. "What?"

"Yep, just as we thought." She looked up. "He has autism."

Tomas grabbed the papers. "Where? Where does it say that?"

"Here." Mel pointed to the words '...diagnosis of a pervasive developmental disorder."

"Where does it say autism? I don't see that."

"Oh, dear." Mel sighed. "This gets tricky. There are a couple systems used for diagnostic criteria. The previous system was from a manual called the DSM-IV. In the DSM-IV, there was sort of an umbrella term of pervasive developmental disorder. Under that umbrella came categories such as Autistic Disorder, Asperger's Syndrome, etc. Under that system, Manny would likely have met the criteria for a diagnosis of Autism Disorder. But the DSM is revised every so many years and the last version came out is the DSM-V. Based on the DSM-V his diagnosis is Autism Spectrum Disorder with accompanying intellectual and language impairments, Level 3."

Maria and Tomas looked blank.

"Although many diagnosticians switched over to using the DSM-V when they diagnose, the team who saw Manny mention terms from both the DSM-IV and V; I guess they were trying to cover all bases. But either way, they say Manny has autism.

"Let's look at this part here." She pointed to a sentence. "Do you mind if I mark on this? "She pulled a highlighter from her purse. "This is the important part where is says, 'confirms a diagnosis of Autism Spectrum Disorder with accompanying intellectual and language impairments, Level 3.'" She underlined those words with the highlighter.

"It's saying that my son has *more* than just autism?"

"Only sort of. He has autism, yes, both going along with the autism is a language impairment; he doesn't talk in comparison to other kids his age."

Tomas and Maria looked at each other. Well, yeah, they had noticed that. It hardly seemed necessary to write that fact down.

Mel continued. "The middle part of the sentence says he has an intellectual impairment as well. His ability to acquire, retain and use information is not the same as other kids his age."

It was quiet around the table as the trio digested the information.

"Can the doctor's fix it?" asked Tomas.

Mel shook her head. "There is no cure for autism. It is a lifelong disorder."

They studied the boys playing in the corner. Every once in a while, two separate giggles could be heard.

Tentatively, Maria tried. "But, Manny, he's changed. He's playing with Kyle and he's never done anything like that before. And you say that Kyle's changed, too."

"Definitely," Mel agreed. "And both boys will continue to change as they grow and acquire new skills."

With hesitation Tomas asked, "Is there a pill?"

"There is no pill that will make the autism all go away. Sometimes some kids are helped by some meds that allow the child to pay attention better or remain calmer so that they are better able to learn, but it is definitely not automatic that if a child has autism, he will take medication."

"What do we do now?"

Mel returned to the report. "After the summary, there is usually a list of recommendations or suggestions. Ah, here they are." She read for a couple minutes. "Pretty standard stuff - exposure to other children, follow the recommendations of a speech/language pathologist, referral to an occupational therapist for follow-up on sensory strategies, social skills training, maintain a language-rich, structured environment, support routines with visuals and work closely with your school."

Looking up, she caught the expression on her friends' faces. "Sorry. Jargon stuff again, but this is stuff I'm comfortable with, stuff we do every day at school. You're in luck. There is not one thing listed here that we don't do at Madson School and do well. You won't need to take time off work to run Manny to appointments; the therapists will come right to the school. And when they're not there, the school staff will carry on with the programming these specialists lay out."

"Who are these people?"

"An occupational therapist is a professional trained in things like life skills and sensory sensitivities. You've already found some sensory strategies that work, like hugging Manny tightly, pressing on his shoulders, using the weighted blanket, etc., but the OT will help you learn more about the parts of Manny's nervous system that might be over- or under-aroused and things you can do to help him stay calm. As he gets older, he'll learn how to regulate himself more, without needing to rely so much on the adults around him.

"The speech therapist will work on a couple things. One is Manny's ability to understand what is said to him. Another is his skills at making his wants and needs known. Some kids show negative behaviors out of frustration when people don't understand what they want. Maybe Manny will eventually talk; we can't know that yet, but in the meantime, the speech therapist will help us work on other ways for him to communicate."

"And all this would happen at school."

"Definitely. All this and much, much more." Mel's encouraging expression contrasted with that of the anxious mother and father in front of her.

Waving plates of gingerbread men under the noses of the boys did the trick. They abandoned their blocks and followed Ellie to a table.

Ben's knees cracked, announcing that he was he rising to his feet. As Ellie started to giggle, he pointed a finger at his sister. "Not a word, you. Not one word." Ellie hid her mouth behind a napkin as she munched on a gingery leg with the little boys.

Ben joined his wife at Tomas' and Maria's table. "Ah, for some adult conversation. What are we talking about?"

"I was just telling them about some of the things we work on at school," replied Mel.

"School is not the way it was when you and I were kids," Ben told Tomas. "I made an ass out of myself with some of the assumptions I had when Kyle started school." Mel nodded emphatically.

"What happened?" asked Tomas.

"What didn't? I hardly know where to start." Ben glanced at his wife. "I bet you can list a whole bunch of things, but I'll recite my sins on my own, thank you." Turning to Tomas, he said, "For one thing, I couldn't get Kyle to school on time. Oh, I'd start way early in the morning, but somehow, it kept not working out and we were late each day, no matter what I did. Mel finally stepped in and her suggestions helped. Still, it wasn't easy.

"Then I made assumptions about some of the kids in the school. I didn't think my son should be around kids who were different. Hell, I didn't want to think that Kyle was different from the average child. I kept denying that he had autism. I know, I know, all the evidence was right in front of me, but I didn't want it to be true.

"I thought that the school was too poor to provide proper desks and chairs, not understanding that they purposely use different types of seating and furniture to benefit some kids. Mel had to explain everything to me, sometimes over and over again. But, she was patient - not! Sure, she has the patience of a saint with the kids, but with me, that's a whole other story."

"Could it be that the kids learn more quickly?" Mel asked sweetly.

Ben pretended to give her a noogie then squeezed her shoulder. "The worst was one of the tantrums Kyle had. I was even there to witness it when my kid ran up to his teacher and kicked her in the shins." Ben ran a hand over his face. "I was getting interested in this woman and trying to make a good impression when my kid attacks her. It's hard to recover from a move like that. But, she forgave me, forgave us, and we moved on."

Maria looked back and forth between Mel and Ben. "Mel was Kyle's teacher?" she asked.

"Yep, that's how we met. Kyle had just come to live with me and I was new to this whole parenting thing, let alone autism. She had to teach both of us."

Tomas was a few sentences back. "Are you saying that Kyle attacked his teacher?"

"Well, I don't know that I'd call it 'attacked'," said Mel. "He was frustrated and he took it out on me. He tended to lash out physically a lot back then."

Tomas turned in his chair to look at his son, Kyle and Ellie. "He seems so calm now."

"Yeah, yeah, but he can still be a little hellion sometimes. He's a kid. But, he's a pretty good kid. It took a while to work out the kinks of how we'd live together, but it's mostly good now."

Maria and Tomas traded glances. They were certainly not at a 'mostly good' stage.

EPILOGUE

The principal had a suggestion. "Why don't you take an early lunch and go home so you can walk your wife and son here for the pizza party?"

Gratefully, Tomas headed home. He and Maria still weren't sure about this decision. So much was uncertain when it came to their son.

As he turned the key in their door, he could hear a woman's voice he recognized, but it was not that of his wife. Maria and Manny sat at the table with their heads together, staring intently at the borrowed iPad screen. As the voice died away, Manny's finger pressed the triangle to make it play again. Mel's voice came through and Tomas recognized pictures of Madson School. Manny was watching the story Mel had made about Manny going to the pizza party.

"Well," Maria stood up. "We're about as ready as we'll ever be." In answer to Tomas's unspoken questions, she said, "It's been a good morning. He's been settled and the sun graced us with the dust motes, so he's nice and relaxed."

As the video ended, Tomas instructed, "Time to get your coat, Manny. We have to leave now if you're going to eat pizza with Kyle."

Marie whispered in his ear, "I'm so nervous, I won't be able to eat a thing."

"Good. That means we'll both have our hands free to jump in, just in case," Tomas whispered back.

They started out, but had only gone half a block when Maria remembered the iPad. It only took Tomas minutes to run back for it. They didn't dare not have it handy, remembering that one incident at the bakery.

Once outside the school, they stopped, showed Manny the door and played the video for him again. Then, taking big breaths, they each latched on to one of their son's hands and entered the building.

The first face that greeted them belonged to Mel. She knelt down to eye level with Manny, gave him a soft hello, and then said, "Give me five." She never let on that her knees were killing her as she waited, then, ever so slowly, Manny's hand rose to brush hers.

Just a tiny bit of tension left Maria's shoulders.

They started down the hallway, bound for Mel's classroom. The sound of rapidly spinning wheels approached them. Tomas' heart sank. As fond as he'd grown of Jordan, he did not want to see him right now. He remembered his initial reactions to Jordan's wheelchair and feared that the apparatus might upset Manny. Before he could interfere, Jordan was there, in all his exuberant glory.

"Hey, Mr. G., watch this!" And Jordan executed his signature wheelie, but with some added flare this time. "Cool, eh?" As his tires touched down, Jordan spun to regard Tomas' family. "Is this your kid?" He wheeled closer, almost on top of Manny's toes. "Hi, I'm Jordan." He held up his hand for a high five.

Manny, who had been mesmerized by the shiny, chrome, spinning spokes of Jordan's chair, didn't move.

Mel stepped in. "Jordan," she called. "What about me?" She held up her hand.

Jordan smacked her hand and grinned.

Mel placed one hand on Jordan's chair to keep him still as she explained. "Manny's new to the school. Let's go easy on him until he gets to know you." She again crouched down to Manny's level. "Jordan wants to meet you," she told him. "Can you give him a high five?"

Jordan, not known for his patience, held his hand suspended. Come on, come, thought Tomas. We only have so long before things can go south on us. The quicker they got this over with and Jordan went on his way, the safer they'd all feel. He moved to reach for Manny's arm, but didn't need to. Manny raised his eyes from Jordan's entrancing wheels and turned his head. Looking out the side of his eyes, he peered at Jordan and raised his hand. Jordan gave it a resounding smack, then with a, "See ya," wheeled away.

Phew. Another bullet dodged.

Then, a small head ducked out of the next classroom. Kyle. "Manny, come on, aren't we ever going to eat? We're waiting for you."

ABOUT THE AUTHOR

Dr. Sharon A. Mitchell has worked as teacher, counselor, psychologist and consultant for several decades. Her Masters and Ph.D. degrees focused on autism spectrum disorders and helping kids to reach as high a level of independence as possible.

In a March 2012 announcement, the Centers for Disease control released their latest statistics on autism. One in eighty-six American children has an autism spectrum disorder and one in every fifty-four boys. Every teacher will have a child with autism in their classroom. Every coach will meet a child with autism. If autism has not touched your family, it will affect your friends or neighbors.

When parents receive the news that their child has autism, they spend countless hours researching the subject, usually at night, after an exhausting day. There is a lot of information out there, much of it by competent authorities. But after a hard day of work and family responsibilities, who wants to read a textbook? Does a book have to be hard slugging for the reader to learn new things? Does learning have to be tedious? What if you could just read a good story and still gain ideas to try? So, the novel *Autism Goes to School"* was born - a light read aimed at a general audience.

Yes, life with autism has it's struggles, but there are strengths as well and the fun parts that any family experiences

There are four more books in this series, each featuring a different child on the autism spectrum. Join the kids and staff of Madson School as they learn and grow and welcome others with special needs into their midst.

ENJOYED THIS BOOK?

If you enjoyed this book, please tell your friends. If you might spare a few moments, the author would be appreciative if you would post a review at http://www.amazon.com/dp/B0184ZQMI6 or wherever you purchased your book.

Author Dr. Sharon Mitchell loves connecting with readers. Contact her through her website at http://www.drsharonmitchell.org. There you will find information on her other books her workshop appearances and questions families and teachers often ask about kids who have autism spectrum disorders.

Would you like to join the author's review team? Team members receive complimentary, Advanced Reader Copies of each new title. Check out http://www.drsharonmitchell.org.

Come back and see how Kyle, Ben, Mel and their friends are doing, and meet more students of Madson School. You'll find them on Amazon at http://www.amazon.com/Dr.-Sharon-A.-Mitchell/e/B008MPJCYA.

Turn the page to see the other books in the series, read a synopsis of each and learn how to get your own free copy.

OTHER BOOKS IN THE SERIES

Autism Goes to School

Autism Runs Away

Autism Belongs

Autism Talks & Talks

Autism Grows Up

Autism Boxed Set - Help for Home and School

Autism Goes to School Workbook (coming in 2017)

Prequel to Autism Goes to School (coming in 2017)

This series began with *Autism Goes to School*. We're thrilled to announce that this Amazon bestseller is also a B.R.A.G. Medallion winner! This is where we first meet Ben, Kyle and Mel.

Get your free copy of this book at this link: BookHip.com/ZPHDQC.

Here's a synopsis of each book:

AUTISM GOES TO SCHOOL SYNOPSIS

We're thrilled to announce that this Amazon bestseller is also a B.R.A.G. Medallion winner!

After suddenly receiving custody of his five year old son, Ben must learn how to be a dad. The fact that he'd even fathered a child was news to him. Not only does this mean restructuring his sixty-hour workweek and becoming responsible for another human being, but also Kyle has autism.

Enter the school system and a shaky beginning. Under the guidance of a gifted teacher, Ben and Kyle take tentative steps to becoming father and son.

Teacher Melanie Nicols sees Ben as a deadbeat dad, but grudgingly comes to admire how he hangs in, determined to learn for his son's sake. Her admiration grows to more as father and son come to rely on Melanie being a part of their lives.

When parents receive the news that their child has autism, they spend countless hours researching the subject, usually at night, after an exhausting day. Teachers, when they hear that they'll have a student with an autism spectrum disorder, also try to learn as much as they can. This novel was written for such parents and teachers - an entertaining read that offers information on autism and strategies that work.

Bonus Section
At the back of the book you'll find links and references useful to parents and teachers.

You can find *Autism Goes to School* FREE at these retailers:
- Amazon.com

134

- iTunes
- Kobo
- BookHip.com/ZPHDQC
- Barnes & Noble paperback
- Barnes & Noble e-book

What Are Reviewers Saying About *Autism Goes to School*?

- "A gem of a book"
- " A true delight - Highly, highly recommended
- Just couldn't put it down"
- "Highly informative and extremely helpful - Couldn't take my eyes off it"
- I loved this book from beginning to end - Just plain awesome
- I could feel the author's passion - What a great way to learn about autism
- "Entertains, entrances & educates: 3 for the price of one!"
- "This wonderful book is about a Dad, Ben, meeting his autistic son Kyle for the very first time, when Mom dumps him suddenly on his doorstep, saying she can no longer take care of him. Through the eyes of Ben, we get a glimpse of both the challenges and joys of being a parent of a child who sees the world in different ways."
- "Unlike some stories that speak of autistic children, this one brings a wealth of hope and information! As we look over Ben's shoulder, we see a glimpse of the learning tools currently being used in the classroom today, and we get glimpses of things that could be helpful in the day to day life of an autistic child."
- "I appreciated this story on several levels. First I enjoyed the story of Ben discovering what it means to be a parent, especially a single parent. Second, I enjoyed watching Kyle find his own means of success in this new and upside down world. "
- "I enjoyed the glimpse into classroom life and options available today. Finally I enjoyed the quiet romance between Mel and Ben."

For a FREE copy of Autism Goes to School go to BookHip.com/ZPHDQC

AUTISM RUNS AWAY SYNOPSIS

Ethan is only in grade one and already has been kicked out of one school due to his tantrums and pattern of running away when in a panic. Now, his mom's enrolled him in a new school but remains glued to her phone, waiting for the call to tell her to come pick him up, that they can't handle him, that they don't know what to do with a child who has **autism**.

How can she trust these strangers to look after her son, just one small child among hundreds, when he has run from own parents so very many times? They don't know the terror of losing your child in a mall or watching him run blindly into traffic.

What started as a fun chase game when Ethan was a toddler has turned into a terrifying deviation. The adults in his life never know when he might take off.

Rather than attaching an adult to his side to keep him safe, this new teacher talks about calming strategies and choices. Do they not realize what could happen if Ethan flees the building? The impact of a car on one small body? Sara is about to learn if this new school is up to the challenge.

Meet Kyle, Mel, Ben and the other characters you got to know in the Amazon bestseller "Autism Goes to School". See what they've been up to in the last year and how they join forces to help Ethan.

Get your free sample chapters at this link: BookHip.com/QKCLG.

You can find "Autism Runs Away" on Amazon at this URL https://www.amazon.com/Autism-Runs-Away-Book-School-ebook/dp/B01FCYQ7DC.

AUTISM TALKS AND TALKS SYNOPSIS

Karen is a grade 6 student who has Asperger's Syndrome. She is bright, vivacious and highly verbal. Too verbal. She finds certain topics fascinating, studies them in-depth and is all too willing to share her knowledge with others. She goes on and on and on, not realizing that she is boring and alienating the other kids with her endless monologues. Her protective mom tries to shield her from the world, limiting her contact with peers in case she might be bullied.

Karen would like to be social. She remains on the fringe, looking at other adolescents having fun together and wondering if she could ever be a part of the group.

Karen has potential. Her inability to read body language and her lack of knowledge in social pragmatics get in the way of interacting with others her age and having friends. Through a structured group at school, she begins to understand the give and take of conversation and to have some positive experiences with her peers.

And, can a young man with Asperger's find love?

Get your free sample chapters at this link: BookHip.com/ LTGFAB.

Find "Autism Talks and Talks" at
https://www.amazon.com/Autism-Talks-Book-School-Daze-ebook/dp/B01IIUZH3S.

AUTISM GROWS UP SYNOPSIS

At twenty-one, Suzie has withdrawn from a world she finds alien and confusing. Ability is not the problem, nor is interest – many things fascinate her. But, she has Asperger's Syndrome and high anxiety. To her, the world is a harsh, scary place where she does not fit.

She spends much of her day sleeping and most of her nights on the computer. Her mother, Amanda, wishes Suzie would get a job, go to school or at least help out around the house. Suzie feels that her time is amply filled with the compelling world lurking within her computer.

Amanda has two full time jobs – one involves working at the office every day, the second involves looking after Suzie. Amanda wants more for Suze, but does not know how to help her move forward. When she tries putting pressure on her, Suzie suffers from paralyzing anxiety, resulting in morose withdrawal or worse, lengthy tantrums. Suzie is most content when alone in the basement with her computer. Staring at her monitor, the rest of the world falls away and she feels at home.

Amanda is torn. She met this gentleman, Jack. It would be nice to spend time with someone other than her brother and daughter but Suzie wouldn't like it and she needs her mother desperately. Amanda's brother asks uncomfortable questions like what will become of Suzie if something happens to Amanda.

Jack gently persists and Amanda glimpses what her life could be like. Suzie resents the time her mom spends with Jack and makes her mother pay for the hours not devoted to her daughter.

Then, they have a home invasion. When an intruder breaks into the house, Amanda has only Suzie to rely on.

Find "Autism Grows Up" at https://www.amazon.com/Autism-Grows-School-Daze-Book-ebook/dp/B01JB8QW3U.

Get your free sample chapters at this link: BookHip.com/ KSGVSC